Skyline 2

Student's Book

Simon Brewster

Paul Davies

Mickey Rogers

MACMILLAN

Contents

Unit			Lesson			Grammar
1	Activate your English	6	1 At an international convention	6		● Question formation
			2 In a foreign city	8		● Review of present simple
			3 Getting to know you	10		statements and questions
			4 Lifeline to international travel	12		
2	Your environment	14	1 A nice place to work	14		● *much, many, a lot of*
			2 A nice place to live	16		● Review of possessive
			3 A big move	18		adjectives
			4 Lifeline to sociology	20		
	Checkpoint 1	22				
3	People in your life	24	1 Family matters	24		● Subject + *be* / *have* + description
			2 Partners	26		● Object pronouns
			3 Love and friendship	28		
			4 Lifeline to psychology	30		
4	Work and play	32	1 Twenty-four hours	32		● Gerunds
			2 Work and gender	34		● Present simple and frequency
			3 Holidays	36		adverbs
			4 Lifeline to stress management	38		● Present progressive
	Checkpoint 2	40				
5	Time out	42	1 On the town	42		● Prepositions
			2 What's on?	44		● Gerunds and infinitives
			3 Party time	46		● *going to* / *will* / *won't*
			4 Lifeline to food management	48		
6	In the past	50	1 Personal history	50		● Past simple *wh-* questions
			2 Growing up	52		● Review of past simple
			3 Crime stories	54		● Past progressive
			4 Lifeline to history	56		
	Checkpoint 3	58				

Functions	Vocabulary	Pronunciation
• Asking for and giving information • Talking about cities • Talking about yourself	• Countries and occupations • Nationalities and languages • International travel	• Sounds - the alphabet
• Giving opinions • Describing places • Talking about accommodation	• The work place • Towns and cities • Describing places • Student accommodation	• Contrastive stress
• Talking about families • Describing people • Talking about customs and cultures • Talking about personalities	• The family • Physical descriptions • Gifts and customs • Personality	• Word stress
• Talking about work and leisure activities • Talking about habits and routines • Discussing current activities • Making definite plans	• Work • Sports and leisure activities • Housework and office work • National holidays	• Weak forms - /dʒʊ/
• Giving directions • Making plans • Making suggestions • Making offers, predictions and definite plans	• Directions • Sport and leisure activities • Parties • Business	• Stress and weak forms
• Talking about personal histories • Talking about school days • Story telling • Talking about events in the past	• Life histories • Crime • History	• Sounds - /ɪər/ /eər/ /ər/

Contents

Unit			Lesson			Grammar
7 Learning for life	60		1 School days	60		• Past simple tense
			2 Choices	62		• Comparatives
			3 Learning culture	64		• *can / could* in requests
			4 Lifeline to career planning	66		
8 On the move	68		1 Getting around	68		• Superlatives
			2 Getting away from it all	70		• *too / either*
			3 Getting there	72		
			4 Lifeline to exploration	74		
Checkpoint 4	76					
9 Healthy living	78		1 Laughter is the best medicine	78		• Possessive pronouns
			2 Your favorite team	80		• *should / need to / have t*
			3 Open wide	82		
			4 Lifeline to living things	84		
10 The story so far	86		1 Turning points	86		• Past tense
			2 Experience and experiences	88		• Present perfect with *ever*
			3 Champions' stories	90		*never*
			4 Lifeline to clothes design	92		• Verb forms
Checkpoint 5	94					
11 Ways of life	96		1 Traditions	96		• *do / make*
			2 Your life	98		• Present perfect with *for /*
			3 Working together	100		*since* and *How long?*
			4 Lifeline to business administration	102		• *tell / ask / want*
12 What's next?	104		1 Reviewing the situation	104		• Review of tenses
			2 Immediate plans	106		• Present progressive, *goin*
			3 Twenty-five years from now	108		*to / might*
			4 Lifeline to communications technology	110		• *will / won't*
Checkpoint 6	112					

Songsheets

Songsheet 1 for units 1 and 2   I say a little prayer

Songsheet 2 for units 3 and 4   The girl from Ipanema

Songsheet 3 for units 5 and 6   Daniel

Songsheet 4 for units 7 and 8   Till there was you

Songsheet 5 for units 9 and 10   The sweetest feeling

Songsheet 6 for units 11 and 12   Holiday

Irregular verbs table
Pronunciation chart

Functions

- Talking about school days
- Talking about plans after graduation
- Making informal and formal requests
- Talking about career choices

- Describing modes of transportation
- Talking about tourist destinations
- Expressing agreement

- Talking about health and giving opinions
- Talking about sports
- Giving advice
- Talking about people's appearance

- Talking about life events
- Asking and talking about experiences
- Describing clothes; giving opinions

- Talking about and comparing traditions
- Asking and talking about people's lives
- Giving orders; making requests and wishes
- Making plans

- Exchanging personal information
- Talking and asking about the future
- Making predictions

Vocabulary

- School
- Applying to colleges
- Career planning

- Transport
- Hotels and vacation destinations
- Explorers and explorations

- Health
- Sports
- Dental health

- Life events
- Auto racing
- Fashion

- Carnivals
- Setting up a business

- Study, work, home, relationships
- Weekend breaks and plans
- Communications and technology
- Connectors

Pronunciation

- Intonation and linking

- Sentence stress

- Sounds - /ɪ/ /i/

- Sounds - vowels

- Stress and rhythm

- Sounds - /eɪ/ /i/ /aɪ/

Unit 1 Activate your English

1 At an international convention

1 Speaking and reading

a Look at the photographs. Answer these questions.

1 Where are these people?
2 Are the people friends?
3 What is the event?

b Complete the conversations.

**WELCOME to the
4th International
Software Convention**
The Grand Hotel, Rome
October 15–18
Registration fee: U.S. $50.00
Please register in the auditorium.
Welcome Cocktail Party:
Thursday, Oct. 15, 9:00 p.m., Ballroom

A: (1).......... .... English?

B: Yes, I do.

A: Hi, I'm José Ramos. (2)......... ....?

A: Peru.

B: I'm Sylvia Daley. (3)......... ....?

A: (4).......... ....?

B: I'm a graphic designer.

c Read the convention welcome notice. Answer these questions.

1 Where is the convention?
2 What type of convention is it?
3 How many days is the convention?
4 Where is the convention registration desk?
5 How much is the registration fee?
6 When and where is the welcome cocktail party?

2 Listening and reading

a Listen to the conversation at the hotel front desk. Complete this form.

b Write questions for the answers. Listen to the conversation again and check your questions.

1 Good morning. .... English? Yes, I do.
2 What's .... ? Rhonda Dubey.
3 How .... your name? R-H-O-N-D-A, Rhonda, D-U-B-E-Y, Dubey.
4 And .... ? The United States.
5 Cash or .... ? Credit card – here you are.

<table>
<tr><td colspan="2">REGISTRATION CARD</td></tr>
<tr><td colspan="2">Guest's name: (1)</td></tr>
<tr><td colspan="2">Nationality: (2)</td></tr>
<tr><td>Form of payment: (3) Cash ☐</td><td>Credit card ☐</td></tr>
<tr><td colspan="2">Room number: (4)</td></tr>
</table>

3 Pronunciation: sounds – the alphabet

a Listen and circle the letter you hear.

1 a h j   3 f l x   5 e i y
2 b c d   4 l m n   6 a e l

b Listen and practice the alphabet.

A B C D E F G H I J K L M N O P Q R S T U V W X Y Z

c In pairs, practice spelling your name. Listen to your partner's pronunciation. Is it correct?

4 Word builder: countries and occupations

a Look at the table. Think of other places and occupations.

Where are you from?	What do you do?	Where do you work / study?
(I'm from) India.	I'm an engineer.	(I work) at a construction company.
China	I'm a doctor.	At the state university.

b Talk to three classmates. Ask questions to complete the table. Ask about spelling if necessary.

Name	Hometown	Occupation	Place of work / study

2 In a foreign city

1 Speaking and listening

a Look at the photograph and answer these questions.

1 Do you recognize this city? What do you know about it?

2 What can you guess about the two people – nationality, age, etc.?

b Listen to the conversation. Are the two people

a) strangers? **b)** friends? **c)** colleagues?

c Listen again and complete the information below.

Name of city: (1)..............................

Location: North coast of California

Main tourist attractions: Golden Gate Bridge, Fisherman's Wharf, Chinatown

Biggest ethnic minority: (2)..............................

Main languages: English, (3).............................. and

(4)..............................

2 Reading

Read the article from *Travel Magazine* and check your answers to exercise 1c.

San Francisco

One of the most beautiful and interesting cities in the U.S. is San Francisco. The city is on a bay on the north coast of California, and tall hills give spectacular views of the city and the bay. Some of the main tourist attractions are the Golden Gate Bridge, Fisherman's Wharf and Chinatown.

San Francisco is a very international city, with ethnic groups from all over the world. The biggest group from one country is the Chinese, but there are also people from every Spanish speaking country. Chinese and Spanish are the main languages after English.

3 **Grammar builder:** review of present simple statements

a **Circle the correct answers.**

1 I live / lives in San Francisco.
2 You is / are from China.
3 She live / lives in San Francisco.

4 We don't live / doesn't live in London.
5 He don't live / doesn't live in London.
6 I am / are not a doctor.

b **Complete these sentences with correct forms of the verbs in parentheses.**

1 San Francisco .... (*be*) in California.
2 It .... (*attract*) tourists from all over the world.
3 The people of Chinatown usually .... (*eat*) Chinese food.
4 Some people there .... (*not speak*) much English.
5 Chinatown .... (*not have*) many French restaurants.

4 **Word builder:** countries, nationalities and languages

a **Look at the examples in the table. In teams, write country-nationality-language sets.**

Country	Nationality	Language
France	French	French
U.S.A.	American	English

Language assistant

Countries, nationalities and languages start with a capital letter: *Brazil, Brazilian, Portuguese.*

b **The teams take turns writing country-nationality-language sets on the board. The team with a correct set of three gets three points. The team with two of the elements correct gets one point. The team with the most points wins!**

3 Getting to know you

1 Reading and listening

a Look quickly at the conversation below and circle the correct answers.

1 Mario and Leo are

   a) friends   b) colleagues.

2 The conversation is about

   a) their work   b) their personal lives.

b Read the conversation again and complete it using the phrases in the box.

> do you like Houston   I hate the weather   do you play tennis
>
> I'm from New York   I usually run in the morning

Leo:	So you're visiting from Colombia, right, Mario?
Mario:	That's right. What about you? Are you from here in Houston?
Leo:	No, (1)........................ .
Mario:	And (2)........................ ?
Leo:	Well, I like the city, but (3)........................ . It's really hot and humid in the summer.
Mario:	Yeah, it is. Leo, maybe you can help me. (4)........................ . Where can I run here in Houston?
Leo:	There's a nice park about two blocks from here. Hey, (5)........................ ?
Mario:	Yes, a little.
Leo:	I play on Thursdays. Do you want to play tomorrow evening?
Mario:	Sure, thanks.

c Listen and check your answers.

2 Listening, reading and writing

a Listen to the interview with Mario and complete the table.

Name Mario Campos	Likes (2)
Hometown (1)	Dislikes (3)
Occupation production manager	Goals for the future (4)

b Read the newsletter article about Mario. There are five errors. Use the information in the table to rewrite the article correctly.

Olson Software Newsletter
New employees

Mario Campos is our new systems manager in Colombia. He's thirty-two years old, and his hometown is Bogotá. Mario likes sports, especially swimming. He swims four kilometers every morning! He also likes going to good restaurants and dancing. He doesn't like going to movies and he hates rainy weather. He wants to travel to Europe someday, and he wants to learn to paint.

3 **Grammar builder:** review of present simple questions

a Look at these examples and then circle the correct answers for the sentences below.

Are you Canadian? Yes, I am.
Is she a doctor? No, she isn't.
Do you work here? No, I don't.

Where do they live? They live in Houston.
Does Mario live in Colombia? Yes, he does.
What does he do in the morning? He runs.

1 For questions and short answers with *I / you / we / they*, use the auxiliary
   a) do **b)** does.
2 For questions and short answers with *he / she / it*, use the auxiliary
   a) do **b)** does.
3 For questions with the verb *be*, **a)** use an auxiliary **b)** don't use an auxiliary.

b Put these words in the correct order to form questions. Add necessary words.

1 live / you / here
2 where / live / you
3 he / what / do
4 like / dogs / she
5 he / where / from
6 you / do / what

4 **Speaking, writing and reading**

a Interview a partner and complete this table.

Name	Likes
Hometown	Dislikes
Occupation	Goals for the future

b Write a paragraph about your partner. Include at least three factual errors! Look at the article in exercise 2b for help.

c Read your partner's article. Underline the errors. Show them to your partner.

4 Lifeline to international travel

1 Reading, speaking and listening

a Read the text and discuss these questions.

1 What countries have a special relationship with your country?
2 What are the reasons for this relationship? For example, do you speak the same language?
3 Do many people from your country go to the U.S.? Why?

Many countries have special relationships with other countries. An example of this is Canada and the United States. They are neighbors and they both began as British colonies. English is the main language in both countries. There is a lot of trade between them, and a lot of tourism.

b In pairs, discuss and mark the sentences T (true) or F (false).

1 Citizens of all countries need a visa to visit the U.S.   T ○   F ○
2 You cannot work legally in the U.S. with a tourist visa.   T ○   F ○
3 There are more than 600,000 illegal immigrants to the U.S. every year. T ○ F ○
4 There is a total of about 1 million immigrants a year to the U.S.   T ○   F ○

c Listen to a radio interview about tourism and immigration to the U.S. and check your answers.

2 Reading

Read the questions. Then find the answers in the information sheet.

Requirements for U.S. travel

1 Where can you get information about requirements
for U.S. travel?
2 What type of visa do you need to go to a conference
in the U.S.?

Getting a U.S. tourist visa

3 Where do you go for a tourist visa?
4 What documents do you need for a tourist visa?

Arriving in the U.S.

5 Can you complete the I–94 form in your own language?
6 What do you do with your I–94 form when you leave
the U.S.?

United States Immigration and Naturalization Service

Requirements for U.S. travel

- Call the American Embassy or Consulate to check visa requirements for your country.
- If you enter the U.S. with a tourist visa, it is illegal to work there.
- You can attend professional conferences with a tourist visa.
- If you are traveling to another country via the U.S., it is possible that you need a U.S. visa. Check this before you travel!

Getting a U.S. tourist visa

- Apply for a tourist visa at your local U.S. Embassy or Consulate. Call to check document requirements first!
- For a tourist visa, you probably need:

  a passport   a birth certificate   a letter from your company
  a property rental or purchase contract   a copy of your bank account

Arriving in the U.S.

- Complete an I–94 form. The airline can give you the form. Write the information in English.
- Go through U.S. customs and immigration. There are usually two lines – one for U.S. citizens and residents and one for foreign visitors.
- Keep your I–94 form. Return it to U.S. immigration officials when you leave the U.S.

  Enjoy your visit to the United States!

---

3 Speaking

In groups, choose an interesting country near your country. Answer these questions.

1 What language(s) do the people speak in that country?
2 What trade is there between that country and your country?
3 What places do tourists visit in that country?
4 What documents do you need to visit the country?

Unit 2 Your environment

1 A nice place to work

1 Word builder: things in an office

a Match the words in the box with the things in the photograph.

> photocopier   telephone   computer
> printer   fax machine   work station

b In pairs, make a list of other things in the photograph. How many things are on your list?

2 Listening and speaking

a Listen to Alison talking to a friend about her new job. What is her opinion of the office?

a) It's fantastic.

b) There are some good things and some bad things.

c) She doesn't like it.

b Listen again. Write a check (✓) next to the positive things in Alison's office.

	Alison	You
space	○	○
attractive design	○	○
natural light	○	○
contact with people	○	○
comfortable furniture	○	○
good equipment	○	○

c What is important to you? Put the list into your order of importance. 1 is most important; 6 is least important. Compare your opinions with your classmates.

3 Writing and speaking

a In pairs, write some good and bad things about your school or workplace.

There's a big cafeteria, but the food isn't very good. There's only one photocopier, and it's old. We need more computers.

b Compare your ideas with another pair.

4 Reading and speaking

a Telecommuting is a new way to work. In pairs, look at these phrases. Which ones do you think apply to telecommuting?

1 People work in offices.
2 Computers are the basis.
3 Workers can live in different countries.

4 It's good for the environment.
5 There are flexible working hours.
6 There is a lot of supervision by bosses.

b Now read the article and check your answers.

Working from home

Work today is very different from the way it was fifty or even twenty years ago. In the past, most people got up early in the morning, traveled to their offices by bus, train or car, worked eight hours and traveled home again.

In today's world, many companies are changing this traditional way of working. More and more people are "telecommuters." This means that they do not commute to an office every day; they work from home. This is possible, of course, because of telecommunications technology like the Internet, the fax and telephone conferencing.

What are the advantages of telecommuting? Imagine you are a telecommuter and your neighbor works for a more traditional company. When he is leaving for the office at 7:00, you're getting up. He is sitting in traffic at 7:30, and you're drinking a cup of coffee and checking your e-mails. At 8:00, when your neighbor is arriving at the office, you're taking a shower. After that, you have breakfast and begin your day's work. You send several reports by e-mail and then you have a teleconference with colleagues in Brazil and Italy. At lunchtime you aren't very hungry, so you decide to continue working. You work until about 4:00, check your e-mails for the last time and take your dog to the park for a run. At six o'clock, you're watching the news on TV when your neighbor arrives home.

c In groups, talk about the advantages and disadvantages of telecommuting.

A: *You have flexible working hours.*
B: *Yes, but you don't have much contact with your colleagues.*

2 A nice place to live

1 Reading

Read the quiz and check (✓) the answers to the questions.

Want to win a trip for two to New York City? Take this quiz.

1 New York's nickname is
a) Crime City ☐
b) The Big Apple ☐
c) The City of Light ☐

2 The population of New York City is approximately
a) 10 million ☐
b) 12 million ☐
c) 18 million ☐

3 In New York, the second language after English is
a) Spanish ☐
b) Chinese ☐
c) Japanese ☐

4 The river in New York City is the
a) Hudson ☐
b) Mississippi ☐
c) Thames ☐

5 New York's baseball stadium is
a) Fenway Park ☐
b) The Astrodome ☐
c) Yankee Stadium ☐

6 New York's basketball team is
a) The Sonics ☐
b) The Knicks ☐
c) The Bulls ☐

7 Broadway is famous for
a) the Stock Exchange ☐
b) designer stores ☐
c) theaters ☐

8 A famous tourist attraction in New York is
a) The Empire State Building ☐
b) The Golden Gate Bridge ☐
c) The White House ☐

2 Listening and speaking

a Mary won a trip to New York in the quiz competition. Listen to her telephone conversation with a friend in New York. Check (✓) the things they decide to do.

○ Go to Coney Island
○ Eat at a famous restaurant
○ Buy presents
○ Go to a museum
○ Have a picnic in Central Park
○ Visit the Statue of Liberty

b What are you probably going to do next weekend? Discuss your plans with a partner.

I'm probably going shopping on Saturday. On Saturday night I'm going to have dinner with my girlfriend.

3 Grammar builder: *much, many, a lot of*

a Look at the rules for when to use *much, many* and *a lot of*.

1 Do not use *a lot of* with singular, countable nouns. But use *a lot of* in all other affirmative sentences. Use *many* in formal English.

*There are **a lot of** restaurants here.*

2 Use *many* with plural nouns in questions and negative sentences.
*Are there **many** restaurants near your house?*

3 Use *much* with uncountable nouns in questions and negative sentences.
*Is there **much** rain in winter? No, the rainy season is in the fall.*

b Now complete this conversation with *much, many* or *a lot of*.

Joe: Are there (1) .... new plans for improvements to the city?

Carol: Yes, but there isn't (2) .... money to implement them.

Joe: Right. And how about crime? Is there (3) .... crime here?

Carol: Of course! It's a big city and most big cities have (4) .... crime.

Joe: You sound very negative about the city.

Carol: I'm not. I love it! There are (5) .... things to see and do – museums, the movie studios and there are (6) .... good beaches and great food! OK, there aren't (7) .... big green areas in the center, but nothing's perfect!

4 Writing and speaking

a In pairs, write a paragraph about a city or town in your country. Don't write the name! You can use the conversation in exercise 3 and the ideas in the circles to help you.

It's a small city. There isn't much pollution or crime. There's a good university and there's a lot of interesting modern architecture.

crime

beaches

public services

interesting architecture

tourist attractions

hot / cold weather

historic buildings

pollution

b Read your paragraph to the class. Your classmates guess the name of the place.

3 A big move

1 Word builder: adjectives for describing places

Look at the photographs. Use words from the table to describe the two places.

Photograph A is a very large, industrial city. It's…

Size	Activity	Appearance	Type
small	quiet	beautiful	agricultural
fairly small	fairly quiet	nice	commercial
large	busy	ugly	industrial
very large	very busy	very ugly	residential

2 Listening

a Laura and her family recently moved from Birmingham, a big city in England, to Avebury, a small town in England. Listen to her conversation with a friend in Birmingham. Does Laura like Avebury?

b Listen to the conversation again. Circle the words in the table in exercise 1 which describe Avebury.

3 Pronunciation: contrastive stress

a Listen to these sentences. Underline the stressed words.

   1 **A**: Is Avebury a big town?   **B**: No, it's a small town.

   2 **A**: She doesn't like quiet places. She likes busy places.

b In pairs, read the statements and correct them.

   A: Birmingham is a small city.

   B: No, it's a big city.

   1 Birmingham is a small city.   **3** Laura likes busy towns.   **5** Paris is an ugly city.

   2 Avebury is a big town.   **4** Kate likes small towns.   **6** We are bad students.

4 Reading

Read the letter and answer these questions.

1   Who is the letter to?
2   What do Laura and her family like
     about Avebury?

5 Grammar builder: review of possessive adjectives

a   Read the letter in exercise 4 again. Who do the words refer to?

1   *our* (line 2)
     a) Kate b) Laura c) Laura and her family
2   *her* (line 7)
     a) the high school b) the classes c) Jenny
3   *their* (line 8)
     a) the boys b) the teachers c) the school
4   *his* (line 10)
     a) John b) the job c) the office
5   *my* (line 11)
     a) the job b) Laura c) John
6   *your* (line 15)
     a) Laura b) Kate c) news

b   Complete this table. Use the letter in exercise 4 to help you.

Dear Kate,

We're in our new house in Avebury. It has three big bedrooms and a nice garden. The children are happy because they can
5 have a dog! The boys' primary school is near our house, and Jenny's secondary school isn't far. She likes all her classes. The boys say their teachers are very strict, but they like the school.

10 John is really happy with his new job, and my job at the gardening centre is going to be very interesting and relaxing. We have nice neighbours, and their children are about the same age as the boys.

15 Write and tell me all your news. I miss you a lot!

Love,
Laura

Singular		Plural	
Subject pronoun	Possessive adjective	Subject pronoun	Possessive adjective
I	my	we	our
you	your	you	....
he	....	they	....
she	....		

Language assistant
Remember, possessive adjectives do not have a plural form.

6 Writing and speaking

a   Write about your ideal place to live.

My ideal place to live is a very large, busy city. It's commercial, but it has nice residential areas. There's a lot of beautiful architecture, and there are many parks and green areas. There are a lot of excellent restaurants and clubs. It's near the mountains.

b   Put the compositions on the wall. Find someone with an ideal place similar to yours.

4 Lifeline to sociology

1 Reading

a Read the first paragraph of the article quickly and choose the best title.

a) A lifestyle decision   b) College life   c) Renting an apartment

b Read the rest of the article and complete it using the phrases in the box.

> **in an apartment**   **at home**   **in a dormitory**

Student lifestyles

Students have to make many decisions – which college to choose, which major to choose, etc. One of the most important decisions is where to live. The three most common options are: living at home with family, living in a college dormitory or living in a house or apartment with friends. We interviewed three students about the advantages and disadvantages of each lifestyle.

Jenny Matthews: "I live (1)_____. I really like it because I meet lots of nice people there. Also, it's on campus, so it's near the libraries and classrooms. We have some supervision, of course, but we also have a lot of independence – not like living at home. And I don't have to shop for food or cook! Of course, it's a little expensive, and some of my friends say I can't really learn about the 'real world' here. But it's fine."

Colin McCloud: "Well, I live (2)_____. I guess I'm less independent than some of my friends, but I want to save money to go to Europe next summer. Also, I have lots of time to study because I don't have to worry about things like shopping, cooking and cleaning."

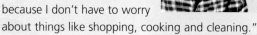

Karen Fisher: "I love living (3)_____. My roommates are my two best friends. It's a little expensive, but I have a part time job to help pay for it. I love being independent and learning to be responsible for myself. Of course, there are some disadvantages. I don't see my family every day, and I have to shop, cook and clean."

Before you decide where to live, consider the advantages and disadvantages of all the lifestyles. Consider your preferences and personality. Talk about the options with your family.

c Match the housing options in the box with the sentences.
There may be more than one possibility.

A **dormitory**   B **home**   C **apartment**

1 Students have adult supervision. A , B
2 They have to travel to and from the college.
3 They have to cook and clean.
4 They meet lots of people.
5 It can be expensive.
6 Students have a lot of contact with their families.
7 They learn to be independent and to live in the
 "real world."
8 It's very convenient for getting to the college.

2 Speaking

a In groups, look at these factors to consider in choosing
student housing. Which four are the most important?

social contacts   study time   adult supervision
distance to college   cost   independence
"real world" experiences   family contact

b Where would you prefer to live: in a dormitory, at
home or in an apartment? Why?

3 Speaking and writing

a In pairs, discuss these questions with reference to your country.

1 Where do most college students live?
2 What factors are most important in this decision? (tradition, money,
 independence, etc.)
3 In your opinion, what is the best option for *most* college students? Why?

b Write a paragraph about college student lifestyles in your country.

In our country, most college students live … They live there primarily
because … In our opinion, the best option for college students is …
because …

c In groups, read the compositions and compare your ideas.

1 Check your progress

a Complete the conversation with the phrases in the box.

nationality are you   do you   your name
do you spell   you speak   old are you

A: Hello. Do (**1**)......................... English?

B: Yes, I do.

A: Good. What's (**2**)......................... , please?

B: It's Takayuki Ono.

A: How (**3**)......................... that?

B: T-A-K-A-Y-U-K-I O-N-O, Takayuki Ono.

A: Thanks. What (**4**)......................... do?

B: I'm a medical student.

A: Really? And how (**5**)......................... ?

B: I'm 23.

A: What (**6**)......................... ?

B: I'm Japanese.

b Read and complete these paragraphs about Takayuki Ono.

Takayuki Ono is (**7**)............ Japan. He (**8**)............ 23 years old. He (**9**)............ in an apartment with two friends. They are students at New York University. Takayuki (**10**)............ medicine. David and Pierre (**11**)............ engineering majors.

There isn't (**12**)............ furniture in their apartment, only three beds, a table, four chairs and two small desks. There (**13**)............ also two computers and a television. Takayuki and (**14**)............ friends (**15**)............ have much time to watch television. They always have a (**16**)............ of things to read or study.

On Saturday or Sunday, they go out and relax. There aren't (**17**)............ good places for an evening out in (**18**)............ neighborhood. But there's a café with live music – jazz and blues. Takayuki (**19**)............ like discos and noisy places; he (**20**)............ comfortable, quiet places.

Score out of 20

◯ 18–20 Excellent!   ◯ 15–17 Very good!   ◯ 12–14 OK, but review.   ◯ 9–11 You have some problems. Review units 1 and 2.   ◯ 0–8 Talk to your teacher.

2 Games to play

a Do the crossword puzzle fast! Then check your answers in pairs or groups.

Clues across
1 The people and language of France.
5 You can eat or write on this.
6 Two times three.
9 The opposite of beginning.
10 A person from the U.S.

Clues down
2 You sit on this.
3 How do you _____ your last name?
4 The opposite of busy or noisy.
7 A place for shopping.
8 A place next to the sea.

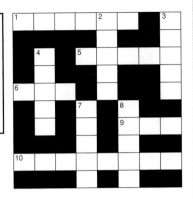

b Work in groups. One student writes a place in your city on a piece of paper (for example, a shopping mall). The other students ask *Yes / No* questions to guess the place.

B: Is it near here?
A: No.
C: Do people eat there?
A: No … uh, yes.

D: Are there stores in this place?
A: Yes.
E: Is it Alfa Plaza?
A: Yes!

3 Your world

a Complete the table with your personal information. Then interview a partner and complete the table with his / her information.

Information	You	Partner
Name		
Age		
Hometown		
Neighborhood		
Occupation		
Place of work / study		
Hobbies		

b Work with another pair. Introduce your partner to the other pair.

This is Ben. He's 20. He's from New York. He lives in Brooklyn. His telephone number is …

4 Personal word bank

Add more words that are important to you. Compare your lists with a partner.

Countries and languages	Office equipment	Occupations	Phrases
Brazil – Portuguese	photocopier	engineer	Cash or credit card?

Unit 3 People in your life

1 Family matters

1 Speaking and reading

a Look at the photographs of two American families. Say how they are different.

b The average American family now has 2.2 children. In groups, discuss these questions about families in your country.

1 What is the average number of children per family in your country?
2 How many brothers and sisters did your parents have?
3 How many brothers and sisters do you have?
4 How many children would you like to have? Why?

2 Word builder: the family

a Read and complete the text with family words from the box.

uncle	sister	daughter	grandfather	children
brother	wife	father	mother	grandparents

In 1970, Mike and Karen were college students. In 1971, they were married, husband and (1)........................ .

They wanted a small family, just two (2)........................ . Their first child was born in 1973, a (3)........................ , Diana. Their son, Peter, was born in 1975. Karen and Mike were good parents. Karen was a strict but affectionate (4)........................ , and Mike was a serious but patient (5)........................ . Diana was also a good (6)........................ to Peter, and he was a good (7)........................ to her. It was a happy and harmonious family.

Most of their relatives lived in the same city. In fact, Karen's sister, Emma, lived on the same street. Diana and Peter were at their aunt and (8)........................'s house almost every day, and their cousin, Veronica, was often at their house.

Two years ago Diana got married, and last year she had a baby girl. Karen and Mike are now (9)........................ . The baby loves visiting her grandmother and (10)........................

b In pairs, talk about your families.

> A: *Tell me about your family.*
>
> B: *Well, we're originally from Maracaibo, and most of my family still lives there. I have four uncles, three aunts and eight cousins there. My cousin, Sergio, studies at the university here, and I see him a lot …*

3 Speaking and reading

a Look at the newspaper article and answer these questions.

1 How do you say "twins" in your language?
2 Do you know any twins?
3 Are they identical twins?
4 Are their personalities similar or different?

b Now read the article and answer these questions.

1 How old are George and Mark now?
2 Who went to Australia? Why?
3 What are some of the personality differences between George and Mark?
4 Are their wives happy or unhappy with them?

Twins meet again after 20 years

Identical twins, George and Mark Preston, met yesterday for the first time in 20 years. Mark left Seattle for Australia at age 18 after a violent fight with his brother over a girl.

"The problem was that I loved Samantha, but she loved George," says Mark. "And Mark was shy and serious, while I was sociable and a bit crazy," adds George.

Mark is now visiting Seattle with his Australian wife, Cindy. "I'm glad they had a fight and Mark came to Australia," she says. "He's a wonderful husband – kind, honest, dependable, and always good company. I really love him."

George is also married. His wife Marie says, "George is a great guy, always a lot of fun, never boring. And he has the most incredible sense of humor – he's really funny!"

So Mark and George are together again after 20 years. And Samantha? "Absolutely no idea," say George and Mark.

4 Speaking

In groups, talk to a partner about your favorite relatives. Ask these questions.

1 Who are they?
2 Where are they from?
3 Where do they live?
4 How old are they?
5 What do they do?
6 Why do you like them?

2 Partners

1 Reading and speaking

Look at the advertisements from a newspaper and answer these questions.

1 What type of advertisements are they?

2 What kind of information do they include?

3 Do the photographs match the descriptions in the advertisements?

■ Section F 14:
Personals

I'm 30 years old, tall and athletic. I have wavy brown hair and blue eyes. I think I'm good-looking! I love riding motorcycles and going to the beach. If you're attractive, 25–30 and want to meet the right man, call Joe at 478–9263.

Single 25-year-old woman seeks man 25–40 who likes music, reading and good restaurants. You have to be sociable and fun, but appearance isn't important. (I'm short and a little fat – not very attractive, but really friendly!) Call Janet, 892–0476.

2 Word builder: physical descriptions

a Use the words in the table to describe the differences between the people in the photographs in exercise 1 and their descriptions.

Joe isn't 30, and he isn't athletic. He's …

Height	Body type	Hair length	Hair type	Hair color	Eye color
tall	heavy	long	curly	black	brown
average height	average weight	medium length	wavy	blond	gray
short	slim	short	straight	brown	blue
				red	green
				gray	

b Write a description of a famous person. Don't write the person's name.

She's tall and slim. She has blue eyes and …

c In groups, read your description. The group guesses the person. Who wrote the best description?

3 **Pronunciation:** word stress

a Look at the words in the box. Answer these questions.

1 Are they similar in your language?

2 Is the spelling the same?

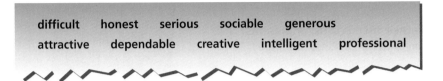

difficult   honest   serious   sociable   generous

attractive   dependable   creative   intelligent   professional

b Now listen and underline the stressed syllables in the words in the box. Then answer these questions.

1 In the first line the stress is on the first syllable. Where is the stress in the words in the second line?

2 Is the pronunciation the same in your language?

c Listen again and practice the words.

4 **Listening**

a Janet is telling her friend Kathy about the man she met through her personal advertisement. Listen to the conversation and look at the photographs. Which man is Janet describing?

A

B

C

b Listen again and complete the table about Janet's new friend.

Personality	Likes
sociable	going to parties

5 **Writing**

a Write an advertisement for a newspaper personals column with information about you and your ideal partner. Use the advertisements in exercise 1a to help you.

b Put the advertisements on the wall. Try to find someone similar to your ideal partner!

3 Love and friendship

1 Speaking

a In your country, when do people give their friends cards or presents? Check (✓) the list. Can you think of any other occasions? Compare your lists in pairs or groups.

○ Their birthday   ○ Their Saint's Day
○ When they graduate   ○ When they marry
○ Christmas   ○ Valentine's Day

b In groups, discuss these questions.

1 When was the last time you gave a card or a present? Who to and why?

2 When did you last receive a card or present? Who from and why?

2 Grammar builder: object pronouns

a Read this conversation. Match the object pronouns (underlined) with the people in the box.

> Judy's boyfriend   Judy
> Judy and Sally   Kathy
> Sally, Judy and Kathy

Judy's boyfriend – him

Kathy: Bobby, can you do me a favor?

Bobby: Sure.

Kathy: Can you pick up Judy and Sally at the airport tomorrow?

Bobby: Judy and Sally? Do I know them?

Kathy: Yeah, they're my friends from Atlanta.

Bobby: I don't remember Sally, but Judy … Yeah, I remember her. She's cute!

Kathy: Bobby, she has a boyfriend.

Bobby: Oh yeah? Well, I'm not worried about him!

Kathy: Well, fine. And Bobby, can you take us to the bus station on Tuesday? We're going to the beach.

Bobby: Yeah, OK, no problem.

28

b Look at the personal pronoun table. Complete the sentences with object pronouns.

1 My boyfriend's name is David. I met
.... at work.

2 My girlfriend's name is Ana. I love
.... very much.

3 My girlfriend gave .... a
present for my birthday.

4 My boyfriend doesn't have money
for presents, but he says "I love
..............," and that is the
perfect present.

5 I bought a present for my wife. I
bought .... at Tiffany's.

6 I also bought some flowers. I
bought .... at a market.

7 We have two children, and they
make .... very happy.

Subject	Object
I	me
you	you
it	it
he	him
she	her
we	us
they	them

Language assistant

In English, you use object pronouns after verbs

She **loves me**, and I **love her**.

and after prepositions

She went to the movies **with me**. I sat **beside her**.

3 Reading and speaking

a Customs for giving wedding gifts vary from culture to culture. Do you know where these customs come from? Read the statements about wedding gifts and check (✓) the correct answers.

1 The groom gives the bride's father a whale's tooth, a symbol of status and wealth.
   a) ◯ Hungary **b)** ◯ Fiji

2 Friends give the bride and groom a horseshoe, for good luck.
   a) ◯ Ireland **b)** ◯ Russia

3 The groom gives the bride thirteen coins, to symbolize his ability to support her.
   a) ◯ Spain **b)** ◯ Hungary

4 Female relatives give the bride purses filled with gold jewelry.
   a) ◯ Fiji **b)** ◯ China

5 The bride gives her friends and relatives candy, and they give her money.
   a) ◯ Ireland **b)** ◯ Russia

6 The bride gives the groom three or seven handkerchiefs. These are lucky numbers.
   a) ◯ Hungary **b)** ◯ Spain

b In groups, discuss the following questions.

1 What wedding gifts are common in your country?

2 Do the bride and groom give gifts to their families or friends?

3 Do you know of any other interesting wedding customs?

4 Lifeline to psychology

1 Speaking and reading

a **Complete this questionnaire. Do you think your favorite colors reflect your personality?**

Check (✓) your favorite color(s).

⬜ ● brown ⬜ ● orange ⬜ ● green ⬜ ● gray
⬜ ● red ⬜ ● yellow ⬜ ● blue ⬜ ● black

Check (✓) your personality.

⬜ calm ⬜ energetic ⬜ full of ideas ⬜ unemotional ⬜ interested in
⬜ logical ⬜ imaginative ⬜ contented ⬜ a leader social problems

b **Read the magazine article and discuss these questions in groups.**

1 What are your favorite colors?

2 Which personality goes with your colors?

3 Do your colors reflect your personality? Why or why not?

The color of your personality

What are your favorite colors – bright reds, yellows and oranges, or more subtle blues, greens and grays? Are you sociable or shy?

Many people think color preferences are related to personality. Scientific research indicates that this theory is correct. Read and see if you agree!

Is there a lot of blue in your clothing and your house? Then you are probably a calm, contented person.

If you prefer beige, brown or gray, you are probably a logical, unemotional person. You like order!

Is yellow your favorite color? Then you are probably imaginative, and like new ideas. You are also usually happy and relaxed.

Do you love parties, people and sports? Are you very energetic? Are you a leader? Then red is probably your favorite color.

Finally, if you are interested in social problems, and you like to help people, green is probably your color. Maybe you are interested in ecology, too.

The psychology of color is important in fashion, interior decoration, marketing and many other areas of life. The colors around you can influence the way you feel and think.

c **Circle the appropriate colors below according to the ideas in the article.**

1 The favorite color of the captain of a soccer team is probably *red / blue*.

2 Probable favorite colors of a scientist or mathematician are *brown and gray / yellow and red*.

3 If you want your office to feel calm, paint it *blue / orange*.

4 Are you shy? For more self-confidence, wear *red / green*.

5 Are you feeling unhappy? Then wear *yellow / brown*.

2 Listening

a **Listen to a conversation between two friends. Answer these questions.**

1   What is Karen's favorite color?   2   What is Donna's favorite color?

b **Read these sentences and circle the best answers. Then listen to the conversation again and check your answers.**

1   Donna is probably
    a) logical and organized **b)** energetic and sociable **c)** calm and quiet.

2   Donna's favorite weekend activity is probably
    a) doing sports **b)** reading **c)** going to parties.

3   Karen is probably very
    a) energetic and sociable **b)** quiet and studious **c)** unhappy.

4   Donna and Karen are
    a) different from their mothers **b)** exactly like their mothers **c)** similar to their mothers.

3 Writing and speaking

a **Write notes about a good friend, boyfriend or girlfriend. Include information about his / her favorite colors, personality and likes and dislikes.**

b **In groups, talk about your friends. Discuss these ideas.**

1   Do you think their color preferences reflect their personalities?
2   Are you very similar to or different from your friend?
3   Why do you think you are good friends?

Unit 4 Work and play

1 Twenty-four hours

1 Speaking and reading

a In your opinion, who usually works more hours: company accountants, hospital doctors or school teachers? Discuss this in pairs.

b Now read the article and check your answers.

The average American

Statistics say the average American works eight hours a day. But "the average American" doesn't really exist, and the differences among real people are enormous.

Joe is a teacher in an Atlanta high school. He works seven and a half hours a day, five days a week. But in addition, he usually works extra hours supervising activities after school and on Saturdays. And he always does some class preparation at home. His real working day is about ten hours.

Marian is an accountant in a Detroit auto plant. She works exactly nine hours a day,

including a one hour lunch break.

Sally is a resident doctor in a Dallas hospital. She often works shifts of thirty-six hours. What does that mean in terms of her average working day? "It means this is a job for young doctors," she says. "It's usually about twelve hours a day."

So where does that "average American" work?

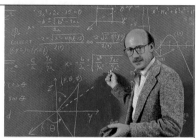

c Complete this table with information from the article.

Name	Occupation	Place of work	Real average working day
Joe		an Atlanta high school	
	accountant		
			12 hours

2 **Pronunciation:** weak forms – /dʒv/

a Listen to these questions, and notice the pronunciation of *do you*.

1 Do‿you study or work?

2 What do‿you study?

3 Where do‿you study?

4 Do‿you study English?

b In pairs, write two other *do you* questions.

c Work with another pair. Ask your questions.

3 **Speaking and writing**

a Work in pairs. Ask questions and complete this form about your partner.

Occupation: _____

Place of study / work: _____

Hours of study / work a day: _____

Starting time: _____

Finishing time: _____

Lunch break from: _____ to:_____

Leisure activities (sports, television, etc.): _____

_____

b Write a short description of your partner's daily routine. Don't write his / her name.

She is a receptionist at the Palace Hotel. She works ...

c Put the descriptions on the classroom wall. Read each description, guess the name of the person, and write it at the bottom of the paper.

4 **Speaking and listening**

a Number the activities in your order of preference in the table under the headings "You." In groups, compare your preferences.

Leisure activities	You	Britain	Sports activities	You	Britain
Listening to the radio			Playing golf		
Watching TV and videos			Playing football		
Listening to music			Playing tennis		
Going to the cinema			Swimming		
Going to cafés, pubs, etc.			Walking		

b Listen to a radio report about leisure and sports in Britain. In the table, number the activities in order from the most popular to the least popular.

c In pairs, check and compare your preferences with British ones.

2 Work and gender

1 Word builder: housework and office work

a Look at this table of expressions for work activities. In pairs, check (✓) the correct column.

	Housework	Office work	Either		Housework	Office work	Either
attend a meeting	○	○	○	do the washing and ironing	○	○	○
check and answer e-mails	○	○	○	talk to a client	○	○	○
cook a meal	○	○	○	wash the dishes	○	○	○
do the shopping	○	○	○	write a report	○	○	○

b Discuss the housework you and others do in your house.

2 Speaking and listening

a Identify the jobs in the photographs. Is there anything unusual in these scenes?

b Listen to two interviews and answer these questions.

    1 What does Mary do?   **2** What does Jim do?

c Listen again, and write Mary or Jim in the spaces. Which job would you prefer?

    1 …........ was an assistant hotel manager.   **4** …........ takes care of the children.

    2 …........ always gets up at five-thirty.   **5** …........ never works on Saturdays.

    3 …........ works from seven to five.   **6** …........ wants to be a very good parent.

3 Grammar builder: present simple and frequency adverbs

a Complete this table with *always*, *never*, *sometimes* and *usually*.

Degree of frequency
0% – .... rarely .... often .... + 100%

b Underline the frequency adverbs in these sentences.

1 Sally often works at night.

2 Jim sometimes enjoys housework.

3 He's always on time for work.

4 Mary doesn't often arrive at work late.

5 She isn't usually home before five-thirty.

6 She never works on Saturday.

c Where is the frequency adverb in sentences with *be* and in sentences with other verbs?

d Write four similar sentences about yourself. Check your sentences in pairs.

4 Reading and speaking

a Answer this questionnaire about housework.

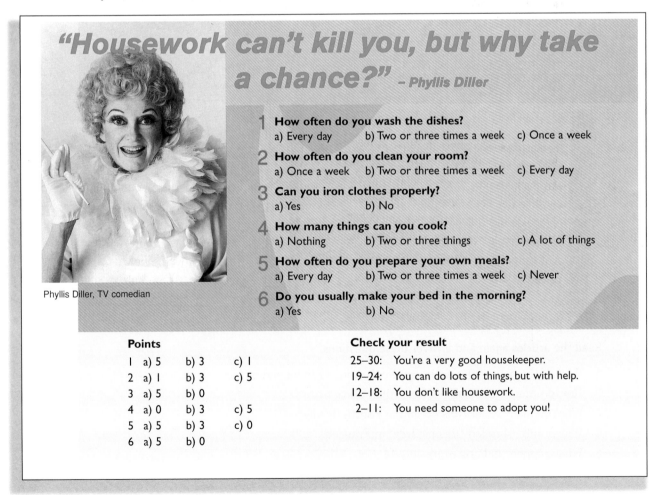

"Housework can't kill you, but why take a chance?" – Phyllis Diller

Phyllis Diller, TV comedian

1 **How often do you wash the dishes?**
a) Every day   b) Two or three times a week   c) Once a week

2 **How often do you clean your room?**
a) Once a week   b) Two or three times a week   c) Every day

3 **Can you iron clothes properly?**
a) Yes   b) No

4 **How many things can you cook?**
a) Nothing   b) Two or three things   c) A lot of things

5 **How often do you prepare your own meals?**
a) Every day   b) Two or three times a week   c) Never

6 **Do you usually make your bed in the morning?**
a) Yes   b) No

Points		
1 a) 5	b) 3	c) 1
2 a) 1	b) 3	c) 5
3 a) 5	b) 0	
4 a) 0	b) 3	c) 5
5 a) 5	b) 3	c) 0
6 a) 5	b) 0	

Check your result

25–30: You're a very good housekeeper.

19–24: You can do lots of things, but with help.

12–18: You don't like housework.

2–11: You need someone to adopt you!

b Compare your results in groups. Is there a big difference between the men and the women?

3 Holidays

1 Speaking and reading

a Describe what is happening in the photographs.

b Read the articles and match them with the photographs.

1

The Bastille was a prison in Paris. On July 14, 1789, the revolutionaries freed the prisoners. It was the beginning of the republic. July 14 is now "Bastille Day," and every year there is a military parade up the Champs Elysées, and public celebrations in every part of the French Republic. A street party and dance are usually part of these celebrations.

2

On July 4, 1776, the thirteen British colonies in America signed a Declaration of Independence. Today, the Fourth of July is celebrated as the national holiday of the U.S. It is celebrated with parades and fireworks displays. But many people are not interested in the celebrations. They go to parks or to the beach to swim, play games and have picnics.

c Read the articles again and answer these questions.

1 What is the date of the American Declaration of Independence?
2 How do American cities celebrate the Fourth of July?
3 What do many Americans do on the Fourth of July?
4 Why is July 14 called "Bastille Day" in France?
5 What happens in Paris every July 14?
6 How do people celebrate Bastille Day in other parts of France?

d What are the main national holidays in your country? What do you do on those holidays?

2 Speaking and listening

a Sue Philips is staying in a Paris hotel. Listen to her telephone messages. Which one is a request, an invitation, a plan?

1 ....
2 ....
3 ....

b Listen again and answer these questions.

1 What is Marsha doing at the moment?
2 What time is the bus to Versailles leaving tomorrow?
3 What does Daniel want?

3 Grammar builder: present progressive

a Look at these rules and examples. Then in pairs, decide the functions of the sentences below.

a) Actions / events in progress at this moment.
   We're doing a grammar exercise.

b) Actions / events extending before and after this moment.
   I'm studying English.

c) Arrangements / definite plans for the future.
   We're having a test tomorrow.

1 Sue is visiting Paris. **b**
2 She is checking her messages.
3 She is taking a trip tomorrow.
4 The bus is leaving at 7:45.
5 We're having a party at the Bastille Restaurant.
6 I'm doing a Masters at the Sorbonne.

b Complete these sentences using the present simple or the present progressive.

1 Sue Philips .... (*like*) France.
2 She .... (*take*) a vacation in France.
3 She .... (*read*) a novel about Monaco.
4 She .... (*fly*) home on July 25.
5 She .... often .... (*not have*) vacations from work.

4 Writing and speaking

a Write some sentences about your current activities and definite plans.

A: *I'm taking karate classes. I'm going to the beach next month.*

b In pairs, read each other's sentences, and ask questions.

B: *Where are you taking karate classes? Who are you going to the beach with?*

4 Lifeline to stress management

1 Speaking and reading

a Look at the pictures and answer these questions.

1 What is happening?
2 How do the people feel?
3 What situations sometimes cause you stress?

b Read the article and complete these suggestions for managing stress. Do you do any of these things?

1 Do ....

2 Spend ....

3 Listen ....

4 ....

MANAGING STRESS

Stress is almost "normal" in modern life, especially for ambitious people living and working in large cities. But it can seriously affect your physical health as well as your happiness. Never accept high levels of stress for more than a short time. Do something about it. Here are some ideas.

Do regular, energetic exercise. This can be a sport, or just walking fast for fifteen minutes every day. Exercise even when you feel tired. Make an effort to spend a little time every week with friends, talking with them, and listening to them. Listen to music, too. It really is therapeutic, and everyone enjoys some kind of music. And finally, meditate. Yes, that may sound strange, but letting your mind float in space can be good for you.

2 Listening and speaking

a Listen to a doctor talking about stress. Is stress a small, medium, big or enormous problem in the U.S.?

b Listen again and complete this information.

1 Percentage of adults with stress-related health problems: ....%

2 Percentage of visits to doctor because of stress-related problems: ....%

3 Annual cost of stress to U.S. industry: $........................

4 Things included in this cost: absenteeism, reduced .... , work
.... , and medical, legal and insurance costs.

c In groups, compare the situation in your country. Use the ideas in the circles to help.

economy   climate   family   crime   diet

3 Reading and speaking

a Answer this questionnaire and check (✓) your results.

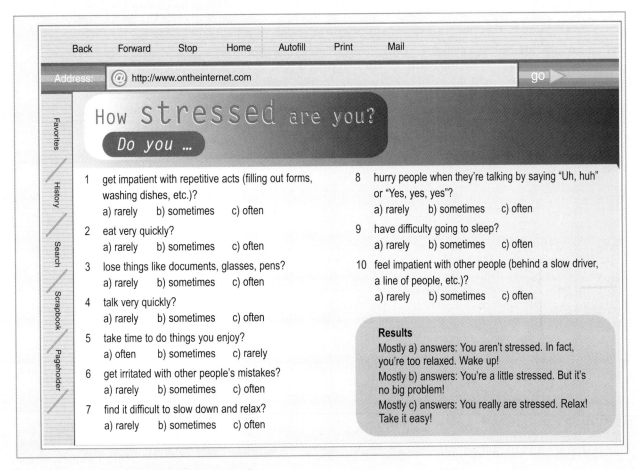

> Back   Forward   Stop   Home   Autofill   Print   Mail
>
> Address: @ http://www.ontheinternet.com   go ▶
>
> Favorites | History | Search | Scrapbook | Pageholder
>
> ### How stressed are you?
> #### Do you …
>
> 1 get impatient with repetitive acts (filling out forms, washing dishes, etc.)?
> a) rarely   b) sometimes   c) often
>
> 2 eat very quickly?
> a) rarely   b) sometimes   c) often
>
> 3 lose things like documents, glasses, pens?
> a) rarely   b) sometimes   c) often
>
> 4 talk very quickly?
> a) rarely   b) sometimes   c) often
>
> 5 take time to do things you enjoy?
> a) often   b) sometimes   c) rarely
>
> 6 get irritated with other people's mistakes?
> a) rarely   b) sometimes   c) often
>
> 7 find it difficult to slow down and relax?
> a) rarely   b) sometimes   c) often
>
> 8 hurry people when they're talking by saying "Uh, huh" or "Yes, yes, yes"?
> a) rarely   b) sometimes   c) often
>
> 9 have difficulty going to sleep?
> a) rarely   b) sometimes   c) often
>
> 10 feel impatient with other people (behind a slow driver, a line of people, etc.)?
> a) rarely   b) sometimes   c) often
>
> **Results**
> Mostly a) answers: You aren't stressed. In fact, you're too relaxed. Wake up!
> Mostly b) answers: You're a little stressed. But it's no big problem!
> Mostly c) answers: You really are stressed. Relax! Take it easy!

b In pairs, compare and discuss your results.

1 Check your progress

a Complete the conversation with appropriate phrases or sentences from the box. Three phrases are not used.

A: Excuse me. (**1**)................................ this sweater?

B: $7.50.

A: Good. Charlie, do you like this? Charlie …? Charlie!!

B: Your son? (**2**)................................. ?

A: He's little – only 5. He has green eyes.

B: (**3**)................................. his hair?

A: His hair? It's red, and curly. Oh, no!

B: Don't worry. (**4**)................................. ?

A: Uh … blue shorts and a green shirt.

B: (**5**)................................. ? Is he sociable, shy?

A: He's very independent, adventurous …

B: Look, is that him?

A: Charlie! (**6**)................................. there?

C: I'm playing, Mommy.

> What are you doing
>
> What's he like
>
> How is
>
> What does he look like
>
> What color is
>
> What does he like
>
> How much is
>
> What's he wearing
>
> What do you do

b Read and complete the e-mail.

Send now	Send later	Save as draft	Add attachments	Signature	Contacts	Check names

To : Mom and Dad

Subject :

```
Hi, Mom and Dad,
Guess what - I'm in love! You don't know Marsha, but you're going to love
(7) _____ , too. She's fabulous, and I'm really happy because she loves
(8) _____! But don't worry - I'm (9) _____ a lot, and I'm going to
graduate. Marsha (10) _____ writing her thesis on astrophysics, and she
(11) _____ to be an astronaut! She doesn't (12) _____ much free time, but
we always (13) _____ out on Saturday, and we (14) _____ go out on Sunday,
too. Hey, what (15) _____ you doing (16) _____ Saturday? Can we visit
you? Can you meet (17) _____ at the bus station? I'll call (18) _____
when we arrive. I want you to meet her because we (19) _____ to marry after
we graduate. We plan to have the wedding in Chicago (20) _____ October. What
do you think? E-mail me soon!
Love, Brian
```

Score out of 20

○ 18–20 Excellent! ○ 15–17 Very good! ○ 12–14 OK, but review. 9–11 You have some problems. Review units 3 and 4. ○ 0–8 Talk to your teacher.

2 Games to play

a Look at the puzzle and try to find the eight jobs.

flight attendant

astronaut

actor

agronomist

personnel manager

waiter

banker

secretary

```
F L Z P A S T R O N A U T L D P
L R P L C T B Q T L P Z U F R E
I Q Z P T L A E N Y X L W R X R
G F D W O F W U D L C D A G V S
H Z F G R T J K O Q R Y I V S O
T B J T X O P Y H X U J T K S N
A G R O N O M I S T H T E L G N
T O V C F J Y W G L E E R D K E
T H N C I L S P W U K A X B J L
E T H W Q K H M Y R V X S R M M
N Y H C P Y C R B J F K W M X A
D D Y J F Y X L A U Q L X M G N
A G L B C R S O N H W Y L S Z A
N Z V J T E S A K U W V R L S G
T Y Z K S E C R E T A R Y W Q E
Z F N M K R Q L R G P V X I Z R
```

b Work in groups. Choose a job and write a brief description. You can use the jobs in exercise a if you want. Read your description to the group. Can they guess the job?

3 Your world

Walk around the classroom and ask about the information below. When a person answers "Yes," write their name.

A: Do you get up early on weekends?

B: No, never.

Find someone who …	Name
1 always gets up early on weekends.	………………………………
2 has a lot of relatives in another country.	………………………………
3 has two brothers and no sisters.	………………………………
4 exercises four times a week.	………………………………

4 Personal word bank

Add more words that are important to you. Compare your lists with a partner.

Talking about relationships	Leisure and sports	Housework and office work	Phrases
uncle	going to cafés, pubs	washing dishes	Red's my favorite color.

Unit 5 Time out

1 On the town

1 Reading and speaking

Read the text and answer these questions.

1 What period of art does the museum cover?
2 What galleries and exhibitions are there apart from sculpture and painting?
3 What services does the museum offer visitors?
4 Which day of the week is the museum always closed?
5 What is the admission fee for people over retirement age?
6 Is it possible to visit the museum without paying?

The **Museum** of **Modern Art**

The Museum of Modern Art is in New York. It is the most important modern art museum in the world. The exhibits extend from the late 19th century to the present day, and include Rodin's "Balzac," Monet's "Water Lilies" and van Gogh's "Starry Night." There are separate galleries for photography, drawing, architecture and design, and the wonderful Tiffany glass collection. The museum also has a restaurant, a cafeteria, a store and a library.

Hours:
Thursday 11:00 a.m. – 9:00 p.m.
Friday to Tuesday 11:00 a.m. – 6:00 p.m.
Closed Wednesdays, January 1,
Thanksgiving Day and December 25.

Admission fee:
Adults: $5.00
Senior citizens: $2.50
Children under 12 (with an adult): free
Thursdays 5:00 – 9:00 p.m.: free
(or voluntary contribution).

2 Word builder: prepositions and directions

Look at the map. In pairs, complete the paragraph with the correct place names.

Donnell Library is in (1)...Manhattan . It's on (2)........................ Street,
across from the (3)...................... . The Museum of Modern Art is between
(4)...................... and the (5)...................... Museum. The Dorset Hotel
is behind the (6)......................... Museum and the (7)....................... .
Donnell Library is near (8)...................... , New York's famous theater street.
From the library, turn left on 53rd Street, go three blocks, cross Broadway and
you're at the (9)...................... Theater. From Donnell Library, turn right,
then turn left at the corner of Fifth Avenue, go two blocks and you're at the
(10)...................... Club. It's on the corner of Fifth Avenue and 54th Street,
on your left.

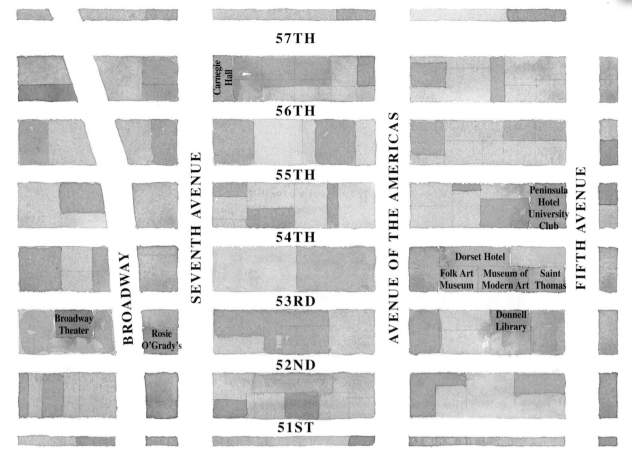

3 Listening

Look at the map and listen to the librarian in Donnell Library giving directions to three people. Write the names of the places.

1 .... 2 .... 3 ....

4 Pronunciation: stress and weak forms

Listen and underline the stressed syllables. Note the pronunciation of *at, of, from, to* and *the, a, an*. Then practice saying the sentences.

1 Turn left at the corner.
2 It's at the end of the block.
3 It's across from a restaurant.
4 It's next to the museum.
5 They're at a concert.
6 It's near an art gallery.

5 Writing and speaking

a In pairs, use the map in exercise 2 to write a conversation asking for directions.

A: *Excuse me. How do I get to …?*
B: *Turn … Then …*

b Act out the conversation for your class.

c In pairs, practice giving directions to places in your area.

2 What's on?

1 Speaking and reading

a Discuss with a partner things you like doing on weekends, for example going to movies, playing basketball, etc. Make a list.

b Look at the advertisements. What is the activity in each advertisement? Which activities are on your list?

1 – dancing

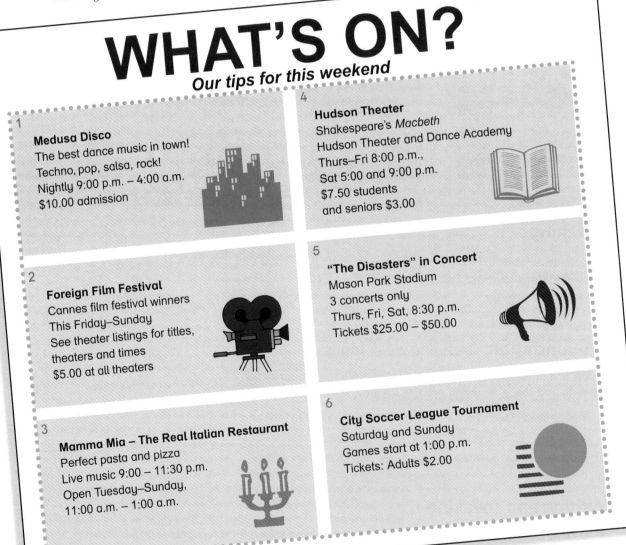

WHAT'S ON?
Our tips for this weekend

1

Medusa Disco
The best dance music in town!
Techno, pop, salsa, rock!
Nightly 9:00 p.m. – 4:00 a.m.
$10.00 admission

2

Foreign Film Festival
Cannes film festival winners
This Friday–Sunday
See theater listings for titles,
theaters and times
$5.00 at all theaters

3

Mamma Mia – The Real Italian Restaurant
Perfect pasta and pizza
Live music 9:00 – 11:30 p.m.
Open Tuesday–Sunday,
11:00 a.m. – 1:00 a.m.

4

Hudson Theater
Shakespeare's *Macbeth*
Hudson Theater and Dance Academy
Thurs–Fri 8:00 p.m.,
Sat 5:00 and 9:00 p.m.
$7.50 students
and seniors $3.00

5

"The Disasters" in Concert
Mason Park Stadium
3 concerts only
Thurs, Fri, Sat, 8:30 p.m.
Tickets $25.00 – $50.00

6

City Soccer League Tournament
Saturday and Sunday
Games start at 1:00 p.m.
Tickets: Adults $2.00

c In groups, look at the advertisements and discuss the type of activity, cost, time, etc. Agree on *one* of the activities for your group.

2 Listening and speaking

a Look at the advertisements again, and listen to four friends making plans for Saturday. Which two activities do they agree on?

b Listen to the conversation again and answer these questions.

1 What is Jenny going to eat for lunch on Saturday? Why?
2 Where are they going to meet on Saturday?
3 What time are they going to meet?
4 Who in the group likes discos?
5 Are they going to a disco on Saturday night?

3 Grammar builder: gerunds and infinitives

a Look at this table and the following sentences. Match the sentences with the categories in the table.

A General likes	B Specific wishes	C Suggestions	D Accepting	E Rejecting
I love eating out.	*I'd like to eat out.	Why don't we eat at Mamma Mia?	Good idea.	*I'd rather not.
I enjoy dancing.	I want to stay at home.		That's fine with me.	No, I don't think so.
		Let's go to the theater.		

Note: *I'd = I would

1 (E) Well, I don't really want to do that.
2 ◯ I'd prefer to go to the concert.
3 ◯ How about going to a movie?
4 ◯ I like watching pro basketball.
5 ◯ Yes, I'd love to see it.

b Complete these sentences with the appropriate form of the verb in parentheses (*to* + verb, or verb + *ing*).

1 Mark loves .... (*go*) to discos.
2 We all want .... (*see*) the new Keanu Reeves movie.
3 I always enjoy .... (*go*) out with my friends.
4 I like .... (*go*) to the beach on vacations.
5 I'd prefer .... (*have*) a cat rather than a dog.

4 Speaking

In groups, make a plan for Friday night. Use expressions from the box in exercise 3a.

Why don't we ...?

Language assistant

- After *would like, would love, would prefer* and *want* we always use *to* + verb.
  I'd like to go home.

- After *like, love* and *prefer* we often use verb + *ing*, but *to* + verb is also possible.
  He loves singing / to sing.

- After *enjoy* we always use verb + *ing*.
  They enjoyed going out.

3 Party time

1 Speaking

a Ask questions to find classmates who like doing these things.

A: Do you always enjoy going to parties?

1 Always enjoy going to parties

2 Enjoy organizing parties

3 Go to one party or more every week

4 Would like to go to a party every night

b In groups, compare your results. Are there any "party animals" in your class?

2 Word builder: parties

a Match the words in the box with the things in the picture.

dancing   beer   sandwiches   potato chips   cards
sodas   stereo   peanuts   cassette   dip   wine

A – dancing

b In groups, describe your ideal party – the people, music, food, drink and activities.

At my ideal party, there are about 20 people. There's a lot of good music –
salsa, reggae …

3   Speaking and listening

a   Listen to the conversation. What are the three friends talking about?

b   Listen again and answer these questions.

1   What two things does Greg offer to do?   3   Does Sandie know Jeff?

2   What two things does Julie offer to do?   4   Why can't Anna come?

4   Grammar builder: *going to / will / won't*

a   Look at these sentences from the conversation in exercise 3. Match the underlined sentences and phrases with the uses in the box.

1 – C

1   **Sandie:**   You know, I'd like to have a party this Friday.

     Julie: Great – oh, but your stereo isn't working, Sandie.

     Greg: Don't worry. (1) I'll bring my stereo.

2   **Greg:**   Jeff Mauldin.

     Sandie: Who's that?

     Greg: He's a teaching assistant in the geology department.
(2) You'll like him. He's really nice.

3   **Sandie:**   OK, and why don't we invite Anna?

     Julie: (3) She won't come because (4) she's going to cook
dinner for her parents on Friday.

A	a prediction
B	a definite plan
C	an offer

b   Complete the sentences with *going to, will* or *won't*.

1   **A:**   Let's go to the concert on Saturday.

     B: Good idea. I .... buy the tickets.

2   **A:**   Why did you buy that paint?

     B: Because I .... paint my bathroom.

3   **A:**   You .... like this salad.

     B: Why not?

     A: Because it has avocados and you hate avocados.

4   **A:**   Nick's a fantastic cook.

     B: Yeah. The dinner at his house tonight .... be great!

c   Match the uses in the box in exercise a with the conversations in exercise b.

5   Writing and speaking

a   You want to plan a party. In groups, write a conversation. Try to include *going to, will* and *won't*.

b   Act out your conversation for the class.

4 Lifeline to food management

1 Speaking and reading

a In groups, answer these questions.

1 Do you often eat in restaurants? Can you recommend any?

2 Do you often eat fast food? What fast food do you eat (hamburgers, hot dogs, fried chicken, pizzas, etc.)?

b Look at the paragraph headings. Then read the article and write the headings in the appropriate spaces.

a) The ingredients of success **b)** The franchise system **c)** Big business

Fast food

I _____

In today's busy world, fast food is very big business. Americans spend more than $100 billion annually on fast food! There are franchises in almost every country in the world. Hamburgers are still the top products, but fried chicken and pizza now represent a large part of the industry.

3 _____

The rapid expansion of the fast food industry is the result of the franchise system. A franchise is the exclusive right to sell a company's products or services in a certain area. The franchiser provides the name, advertising, the product, staff training and quality control. As an example of the effectiveness of franchising, in the 1980s McDonald's opened a new restaurant somewhere in the world every seventeen hours!

2 _____

Why is fast food so successful? First, because it offers a limited menu, which reduces costs and facilitates quick service. Second, fast food companies have enormous numbers of restaurants, so they are very well-known and easily accessible. Finally, for people in a hurry, fast food offers a quick, cheap eating option.

c Read the article again and complete these notes.

1	Annual spending on fast food in the U.S.	$100 billion
2	The most popular fast food product	
3	Advantages of offering a limited menu	
4	Advantages of having a large number of restaurants	
5	Definition of "franchise"	
6	What the franchiser offers the franchisee	

2 Speaking and writing

a Imagine you are going to start a new fast food business. Look at this list of steps for starting a business, and number them in order. In pairs, compare the order you chose.

- ◯ Plan an advertising campaign.
- ◯ Study the market opportunities and the competition.
- ◯ Find a suitable location.
- ① Decide on and "design" a product and service.
- ◯ Calculate the income, the costs, and the profit margin.

b In pairs, complete this table with ideas for your fast food business.

Type(s) of food	Main type(s) of customer	Differences from competition
healthy fast food		

c Work in pairs and write a short proposal for your new business.

Our business, "Bunny Buns," will sell rabbit hamburgers. We will have our own rabbit farm.

d Put your proposal on the wall. Vote for the best proposal (*not* your own!).

49

Unit 6 In the past

1 Personal history

1 Speaking and reading

a What do you know about the man in the photographs below?

b Match the topics with the paragraphs in the article.

 a) The accident   c) His life today

 b) His childhood   d) His education and big opportunity

A Real Superman

Everyone knows the fictional Superman. This is the story of a real one.

1 (b)
Christopher Reeve was born in New York on September 25, 1952. As a boy he loved sports. He also liked the theater and movies.

2 ○
He graduated from Cornell University, and then studied drama at the Julliard School in New York. For several years, he acted in plays and television soap operas. His big break in the movies came in 1975. He was chosen from more than 200 actors to play Superman!

3 ○
Christopher became a big movie star. As a hobby, he began riding

horses, and became good at it. He was competing in a jumping event on May 27, 1995, when he fell and hit his head. He was paralyzed from the neck down.

4 ○
At first, he didn't want to live. But then he began to make a great effort to accept life in a wheelchair. He can't move his body, but he is very active now! He still acts, and is a director, too. He also travels a lot representing paralyzed people in the U.S. In 1996, he established the Christopher Reeve Foundation to promote research on paralysis.

c Read the article again and complete the profile.

Profile of Christopher Reeve	
Date / place of birth	
Favorite activities as child	
Education	
Date / character of big movie role	
Date / type of accident	
Present activities	
Starting date / purpose of foundation	

2 Pronunciation: sounds – /iər/, /eər/, /ər/

a Listen to the pronunciation of *we're, where* and *were* and then the words 1–6. Write the words in the correct columns in the table.

| 1 | beer | 3 | hair | 5 | sir |
| 2 | her | 4 | here | 6 | wear |

we're /iər/	where /eər/	were /ər/
....	....	....
....	....	....
....	....	....

b Listen to these questions and answers. Ask different people the questions.

1 *A: Where's your family from?*
  B: We're from Chicago mostly.

2 *A: Where were you born?*
  B: I was born in Boston.

3 Writing and speaking

a Write notes about yourself.

Date / place of birth	
Place(s) where you grew up	
Likes / dislikes as child	
Education (schools / college, etc.)	
Major illnesses / accidents	
Important people in your past	

b In pairs, talk about your personal histories. Ask your partner questions and take notes.

Where did you grow up?

c Use your notes to write a short biography of your partner. Put it on the wall. Read the other biographies, and find two which have similarities to your life.

d Try to write one fact from the biographies of as many people in your class as possible. Then check the facts with your classmates.

Stephanie changed schools when she was six.

2 Growing up

1 Speaking and writing

a Describe and discuss these photographs.

b List three memorable things you did when you were about 16. In groups, compare your lists.

2 Listening

a Listen to a high school student interviewing two people about their school days. What are they doing now?

b Listen to the interview again and complete this table.

Name	Favorite subjects	Ambition(s)	Taste(s) in music	First love
Jenny Ford				

Name	Favorite subjects	Ambition(s)	Taste(s) in music	First love
Alex Young				

3 Grammar builder: review of past simple

a   In pairs, copy and complete this table on a piece of paper. Put your completed
    table on the wall. The first pair with a correct table wins.

Infinitive	Past	Infinitive	Past	Infinitive	Past
1 begin	began	9 get		17 meet	
2 buy		10 give		18 see	
3 come		11 go		19 spend	
4 do		12 grow		20 read	
5 drive		13 have		21 say	
6 eat		14 hear		22 take	
7 fall		15 leave		23 win	
8 fly		16 make		24 write	

b   Complete the article with the correct verbs in the past simple.

Voices from the past

Our reporter, Karen Hadley, talked to some former Boston High students. What were they like then? What are they like now? Read this to find out.

Jenny Ford (1)_____ up in Boston and graduated from Boston High in 1985. She said she (2)_____ sociology and she loved history. When she

(3)_____ in high school, she loved rock music and she (4)_____ to be a rock musician. She (5)_____ guitar and (6)_____ in a band. But she (7)_____ become a rock star! She became a very successful lawyer.

And what about boyfriends? Jenny (8)_____ in love with Alex

Young when she was sixteen. But that was a long time ago. In 1995, she (9)_____ Paul Harris. They (10)_____ married in 1997. Now they have two children and they live near Boston.

4 Speaking and writing

a   In pairs, talk about when you were in high school. Write your partner's
    information in this table.

Name	Favorite subjects	Ambition(s)	Taste(s) in music	First love	Other information

b   Now use the information to write a short paragraph about your partner's high
    school days. Use the article in exercise 3b for ideas.

c   Tell another pair about your partner. Your partner corrects any incorrect
    information. The other pair can ask for more information if they want to.

3 Crime stories

1 Speaking and reading

a Look at the newspaper headlines and the picture. Which title is correct?

    a) Bank Robbed by Wild Bunch

    b) Wild Bunch Escapes from Jail

    c) Wild Bunch Steals Railroad Payroll

b Read the extract from "Train Robbers." Number the events in the correct order.

    ◯ They robbed the passengers.

    ◯ They escaped on horseback.

    ◯ A gang was waiting near Wilcox.

    ◯ They stopped the train with a tree.

    (1) A Union Pacific train was traveling west.

    ◯ They dynamited the safe.

TRAIN ROBBERS

Butch Cassidy, the Sundance Kid and the Wild Bunch

On June 2, 1899, a Union Pacific train was traveling west, and the passengers were talking, reading or sleeping. The train was carrying a payroll for railroad employees. Near Wilcox, Wyoming, a gang called the Wild Bunch was waiting. Their leaders were the notorious robbers Butch Cassidy and the Sundance Kid. The gang stopped the train with a tree across the track. They took money, watches and jewelry from the passengers. But they really wanted to steal the payroll. They used dynamite to open the express car, but they used too much

dynamite on the safe and blew money all over the area. The Wild Bunch escaped on their horses with $30,000. When the authorities arrived, some passengers were still looking for bank notes.

c Read the newspaper extract again and complete this fact sheet.

Date of robbery	
Railroad company	
Place of robbery	
Name of gang	
Method of opening safe	
Amount of money stolen	

Language assistant

In English, you *rob* a person or place (bank, store), but you *steal* money or things (jewelry, a car).

2 **Grammar builder:** past progressive

a **Look at the rule for using the past progressive. Which of the sentences is an example of a) and which of b)?**

We use this tense to talk about something in progress around a certain time in the past. We often:

a) specify the time, *or* **b)** mention an event, using the past simple.

1   Passengers were looking for bank notes when the authorities arrived.

2   An hour later, the robbers were celebrating in their hideout.

b **Circle the appropriate forms (past progressive or past simple) in these sentences.**

1   Some passengers *had / were having* lunch when the train
    stopped / was stopping.

2   When the robbers *got / were getting* on the train, the guard
    slept / was sleeping.

3   Nobody *saw / was seeing* the robbers' faces because they
    wore / were wearing masks.

3 **Speaking and listening**

a **In pairs, look at the picture and discuss what happened in the store.**

b **Listen to a policewoman questioning two witnesses. Complete this table.**

	Witness 1	Witness 2
Time of robbery	....	....
Number of robbers	....	....
Number of men / women	....	....

c **Which witness gave the correct information?**

4 **Speaking**

a **Read this text.**

Last night between 9 and 12, a car was stolen from outside this building. The police suspect two students in this class. They want to question them. The students are … (your teacher will tell you!)

b **The suspects leave the class. They agree about their activities together between 9 and 12 last night. The other students prepare questions. Use the phrases in the circles to help you.**

c **One of the suspects returns and the class questions him / her. Then the second suspect returns for interrogation. Contradictions between the suspects' stories mean they will go to prison!**

their
activities

people
they saw

their
clothes

where the
suspects
went

4 Lifeline to history

1 Reading and speaking

Match the dates to the newspaper headlines.

1	1917	**a)**	President Kennedy Assassinated!
2	1939	**b)**	Thatcher First Woman Prime Minister in Europe!
3	1963	**c)**	Clinton on Trial!
4	1969	**d)**	Revolution in Russia!
5	1979	**e)**	War in Europe to Stop Hitler!
6	1998	**f)**	Man on the Moon!

2 Reading and speaking

In groups, play the history game. You need a dice and a marker.

1 One student is the referee. He / she looks at the answers on page 57.

2 Roll the dice and move your marker the corresponding number of spaces.

3 Answer the question on the space. If your answer is correct, stay on the space. If your answer is incorrect, go back to your previous space.

4 The first player to go from "In the Beginning" to "Now" wins!

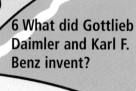

6 What did Gottlieb Daimler and Karl F. Benz invent?

5 Who liberated northern South America from Spain?

4 Who was the first U.S. president?

3 What did Sony invent in 1982?

2 When did Columbus arrive in the Americas?

1 What great city was founded in 753 B.C.?

IN THE BEGINNING!

7 Who invented the telephone?

8 Where were the first modern Olympic Games held?

9 When did the Berlin Wall come down?

10 When did the U.S. return the Panama Canal to Panama?

11 Who was Mahatma Gandhi?

12 When was the first soccer World Cup?

now

20 Who was Joan Miró?

19 Who discovered radium?

18 Who painted the Mona Lisa?

17 What royal wedding took place in 1981?

16 Who wrote *One Hundred Years of Solitude*?

15 Where was President Kennedy assassinated?

14 Which country sent the first man into space?

13 When did World War II end?

10:57

3 Writing and speaking

a Write at least three questions about well-known events or people in your country. They can be *Yes / No* questions (*Did ...?*) or information questions (*Who ...? When ...? Where ...? What ...?*).

b In groups, take turns asking the questions you have prepared. The person with the most correct answers wins.

Answers to board game in exercise 2

1 Rome
2 1492
3 The CD player
4 George Washington (1789–1797)
5 Simón Bolívar (1819–1821)
6 The gasoline powered automobile
7 Alexander Graham Bell (1876)
8 Athens, Greece (1896)
9 1989
10 December 31, 1999

11 An Indian political leader (early 20th century)
12 1930
13 1945
14 The Soviet Union (1961)
15 Dallas, Texas (November 22, 1963)
16 Gabriel García Márquez (1967)
17 Prince Charles and Lady Diana Spencer
18 Leonardo da Vinci (1503–1506)
19 Marie Curie (1898)
20 A Spanish surrealistic painter (early 20th century)

Checkpoint 3

1 Check your progress

a Read this conversation. Complete it with appropriate forms of the verbs in parentheses.

Robert: How about (**1**)........................ (*go*) out tonight?

Susan: Sure. What do you want (**2**)........................ (*do*)?

Robert: Why don't we (**3**)........................ (*try*) the new disco, Midnight? It's salsa night.

Marcy: Good idea. I'd like (**4**)........................ (*see*) it.

Susan: Me too. I love (**5**)........................ (*dance*)!

Brandon: Where's the disco?

Robert: It's near Walmart. You (**6**)........................ (*turn*) right on the next corner.

Marcy: Then it's two blocks down.

Brandon: Ah, yes, I know. Oh no! I can't (**7**)........................ (*go*) tonight.

Susan: Why not?

Brandon: I have (**8**)........................ (*study*) for an exam.

Marcy: That's too bad.

Brandon: Yeah. I really enjoy (**9**)........................ (*listen*) to Latin music but this exam is very important.

Marcy: Look. Let's (**10**)........................ (*meet*) for coffee tomorrow night after your exam. We can go to Midnight next week.

Brandon: Sure. See you tomorrow. Bye!

b Susan went out with Robert. Read the e-mail she wrote to her friend Carol. Complete the e-mail.

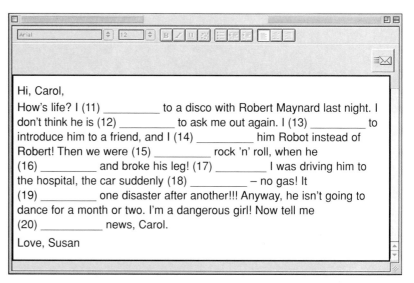

Hi, Carol,

How's life? I (11) _____ to a disco with Robert Maynard last night. I don't think he is (12) _____ to ask me out again. I (13) _____ to introduce him to a friend, and I (14) _____ him Robot instead of Robert! Then we were (15) _____ rock 'n' roll, when he (16) _____ and broke his leg! (17) _____ I was driving him to the hospital, the car suddenly (18) _____ – no gas! It (19) _____ one disaster after another!!! Anyway, he isn't going to dance for a month or two. I'm a dangerous girl! Now tell me (20) _____ news, Carol.

Love, Susan

Score out of 20

18–20 Excellent! 15–17 Very good! 12–14 OK, but review. 9–11 You have some problems. Review units 5 and 6. 0–8 Talk to your teacher.

58

2 Games to play

a Work in groups. One student writes the name of a place in your city on a piece of paper, and then gives directions there. The others try to guess the place.

A: *Turn right outside this building. Go four blocks and turn left …*

B: *Is it the zoo?*

A: *No, it isn't. Turn left and walk past the zoo. Cross Washington Avenue and …*

C: *Is it …?*

b Work in groups. One student writes the name of a resort or vacation center on a piece of paper, and then describes plans for a vacation there. The others try to guess the place.

A: *I'm going to swim and sunbathe a lot. I'm going to eat French food. I'm going to see famous people, maybe a princess …*

B: *Is it Monaco?*

A: *Yes, it is!*

3 Your world

a In pairs, plan a weekend for a visitor to your town or city. Money is no problem! Organize a party and include these ideas in your plan: movies, live music, dancing and sports.

b Tell another pair about your plans. Combine the best ideas from both plans to create a super weekend in your town or city.

4 Personal word bank

Add more words that are important to you. Compare your lists with a partner.

Food and drink	Entertainment	Location	Phrases
soup	going out	on the corner of	Let's go to a movie.

Unit 7 Learning for life

1 School days

1 Word builder: school vocabulary

Number the words in the correct category: Put 1 for "Subjects," 2 for "People."

(2) administrator	( ) classmate	( ) history	( ) physics
(1) biology	( ) coach	( ) janitor	( ) principal
( ) captain	( ) computing	( ) literature	( ) student
( ) chemistry	( ) geography	( ) math	( ) teacher

2 Speaking

a Complete this information about your high school.

Your favorite:	Your least favorite:
subject	subject
teacher	teacher
classmate	classmate

b In groups, discuss the information above.

Who was your favorite teacher?

3 Speaking and reading

Look at the reports on page 61. Then write the correct name, Jennifer or Anita, in the teacher's comments below.

1

_____ has good and bad areas. She has great ability and interest in science subjects, but needs to make more effort at subjects that are more difficult for her. She has the intelligence, and just needs to make the same effort as in sports!

2

_____ is a good student in general. She makes an effort even in difficult subjects for her, like the sciences. Language and literature are possible majors for her at college. She did very good work as assistant editor of the school magazine.

\multicolumn{3}{l}{**Barndale High School Report**}		
Student: Jennifer Ocampo	
Subject	**Grade**	**Comments**
Math	B+	Very good work all year
History	C-	Not really interested
English literature	D	Didn't read or study at all
Geography	C+	Satisfactory; better than last year
Physics	A	Excellent work!
Computer science	A-	Has ability in this subject
French	C-	Doesn't like the language; needs to practice more
Sports	A	Captain of girls' soccer team, and on basketball team
Overall grade B		

Date: 20/6/95 Signed: *Mrs Newmarch*

\multicolumn{3}{l}{**Barndale High School Report**}		
Student: Anita Garner	
Subject	**Grade**	**Comments**
Math	C	Has difficulty with math, but works hard
History	B	Did good work this year
English literature	A	Has talent in this area
Geography	C+	Satisfactory
Physics	C	Trying hard, and improving
Computer science	B	Good work
French	A-	Better and better!
Sports	B-	Substitute on the girls' softball team
Overall grade B		

Date: 20/6/95 Signed: *Mrs Newmarch*

4 Listening, writing and speaking

a Listen to a school principal interviewing a woman for a teaching job. Is the applicant Jennifer or Anita?

b Listen again and complete the principal's notes.

Graduated from Barndale High School in
(**1**)........................ Majored in
(**2**)........................ at Georgia State
University.
Teaching experience: (**3**) ....
Interests: (**4**) ....

c Use the interview notes in exercise b to complete the principal's report on the applicant. In groups, compare your information. Is she a good applicant or not?

Report on interview with (**1**)...

The applicant interviewed for a job as (**2**)... She has a

degree in (**3**)............................... from (**4**).. Her work

experience is (**5**)................................. She is interested in

(**6**)................................. I think (**7**).. .

2 Choices

1 Speaking and listening

a Here are some things people do after graduation from high school. In groups, talk about what you did after high school.

1 do volunteer work
2 go to university
3 start work
4 travel
5 take a vocational training course
6 get married

b Listen to some high school students talking about their plans with their teacher. Recommend options for Jodie, Pamela, Neil and Chuck.

I think Jodie should ...

2 Reading

a Pamela's teacher gave her two leaflets. Read them and complete Pamela's summary table.

	Year founded	Number of students / staff	Fees per year
MIT			
UCLA			

Massachusetts Institute of Technology

Massachusetts Institute of Technology (MIT) was founded in 1861. It is one of several highly prestigious educational and research institutions in the Boston area. MIT has about 10,000 students, and more than 900 faculty members. Tuition fees vary, but are about $25,000 a year. Scholarships are available, and ...

The University of California at Los Angeles (UCLA) was founded in 1882. Today it is one of the nation's largest universities, with over 35,000 students and almost 2,000 faculty members. Tuition fees range generally between $17,000 and $20,000 per year. Scholarships ...

b Pamela's teacher also left her a note. Which university is she recommending? What will Pamela need to do to go to the recommended university?

Pamela,
I hope these leaflets will help. I went to UCLA, but I'll try to be neutral. MIT is probably better for you. Boston is colder than Los Angeles in the winter, so it's good for staying home and studying! But seriously, I think it's the right place for you. Unfortunately, it's more expensive than most universities, so you may need to try for a scholarship.
Ruth

3 **Grammar builder:** comparatives

a Underline the adjectives in these sentences. Which other sentences
are like sentence 1 and which are like sentence 2?

1 Boston is **colder than** Los Angeles.
2 MIT is **more expensive than** UCLA.
3 UCLA is bigger than MIT.
4 MIT is more exclusive than UCLA.
5 Harvard is more famous than MIT or UCLA.
6 Boston is smaller than Los Angeles.

b Complete these sentences with comparative forms.

1 Boston is .... (*old*) Los Angeles.
2 Los Angeles is .... (*modern*) Boston.
3 The climate in Boston is .... (*extreme*) in
  Los Angeles.
4 UCLA is .... (*cheap*) MIT.
5 Pamela is .... (*intelligent*) her classmates.
6 Simon is .... (*young*) his brother Paul.

> **Language assistant**
> ● Two-syllable adjectives ending in -y
> after a consonant: Change -y to -i
> and add -er. pret**ty** – prett**ier**,
> hap**py** – happ**ier**.
> ● There are some irregular adjectives:
> good – better, bad – worse.

4 **Speaking and writing**

a Compare Canada and Jamaica. Use adjectives from the circles or your own ideas.

Canada is more industrialized than Jamaica.
Jamaica is a poorer country than Canada.

big   exotic   small   cheap   expensive   developed

dangerous   cosmopolitan

warm   poor   industrialized

cold   pretty

modern

b Would you prefer to learn English in Canada or Jamaica?
Write reasons for your choice. In groups, read and discuss
your reasons and choices.

3 Learning culture

1 Grammar builder: *can / could* in requests

a Read the conversations and match them with the speakers in the box.

> A **husband and wife**   B **friends**   C **colleagues**

1 – A, B, C

1 A: Oh, I forgot to go to the bank! Could you lend me $5.00?
   B: Of course, no problem.

2 A: Can I use your dictionary?
   B: Sure. Here it is.

3 A: Can you get some bread when you go to the store?
   B: Sure.

4 A: Could I talk to you after the meeting?
   B: Yes, at about 3:00.

5 A: Do you mind if I give you my report tomorrow, Mr. Bloom?
   B: That's fine.

b In pairs, decide which requests in exercise a are informal and which are formal.

1 – formal or informal

2 Listening

a Grace Clark works for a university. Listen to her five telephone messages and say if they are personal or professional.

1 – professional

b Listen to the telephone messages again and match them with Grace's notes.

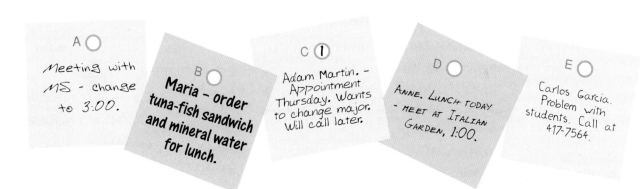

A ◯
Meeting with MS - change to 3:00.

B ◯
Maria – order tuna-fish sandwich and mineral water for lunch.

C ①
Adam Martin. - Appointment Thursday. Wants to change major. Will call later.

D ◯
ANNE. LUNCH TODAY - MEET AT ITALIAN GARDEN, 1:00.

E ◯
Carlos Garcia. Problem with students. Call at 417-7564.

3 Pronunciation: intonation and linking

a Listen to these sentences. Is the intonation rising or falling?

1 Could I come and see you on Thursday?
2 Do you mind if we meet at 3 o'clock?
3 Can I meet you at the restaurant?
4 Could you call me right away?
5 Can you order me a sandwich?
6 Would you like a drink?

b Listen again. How do the underlined words sound? Practice saying the sentences.

4 Reading and speaking

a Imagine you are studying or working in an English-speaking country. Read this quiz and answer the questions.

How polite are you?

Take this cultural competence quiz to find out!

I You are visiting friends and you want to smoke. Would you …

a) say "Would you like a cigarette?" ☐
b) light your cigarette? ☐
c) say "Do you mind if I smoke?" ☐

2 You're watching TV with good friends. The room is very hot. Would you …

a) open a window? ☐
b) say "Can I open a window?" ☐
c) say "Do you mind if I open a window?" ☐

3 You're in a shoe store. You say to the clerk …

a) "Could I see these shoes in size 7?" ☐
b) "Do you mind if I see these shoes in size 7?" ☐
c) "I want to see these shoes in size 7." ☐

4 You are living with a family. You want to use their washing machine. Would you …

a) say "Do you mind if I use your washing machine?" ☐
b) say "I want to use your washing machine, please." ☐
c) use the machine? ☐

b In groups, talk about the answers. Then look at the box. Who's the most culturally competent person in your group?

Answers:
1 – c; 2 – b; 3 – a; 4 – a

5 Speaking

In groups, decide what you would say in these situations.

1 You want to ask a store clerk for change for a ten-dollar bill.
2 You're eating dinner with your host family. You want someone to pass the salt.
3 You want to borrow your friend's new car.
4 You want to ask your boss for a day off work.

4 Lifeline to career planning

1 Reading and speaking

a Discuss these questions.

  1 Do you work or study? Where do you work or what do you study?

  2 Why did you choose your job or area of study?

b In the article below there is information about specific career areas in reference to the U.S. Which of the careers in the box do you think are growing the fastest?

---

law   computing and data processing   home health care   construction and architecture

management and public relations   education   automotive services   sanitary services

---

c Read the article and check your answers.

Career planning

How does a person decide what course of study to take in college and what career to choose afterwards? It's a difficult decision, but you should consider factors which are important to you personally and then find out as much as possible about different career areas. If a high salary is important, you might want to consider a career in law or business. If you are more interested in personal satisfaction, perhaps a career in teaching or the arts is best for you.

It is useful to find out which career areas are growing in your area. For example, in the U.S. the fastest growing industry is, of course, computing and data processing. Other areas of fast growth are home health care, automotive services, sanitary services, management and public relations, freight transportation and personnel services. Relevant college degrees are computer science, medicine and business administration.

But not every career requires a college degree. People who work in home health services, sanitary services or transportation, for example, need technical training. Finally, experts say you will probably change jobs at least three times in your life, so be open to change!

d Read the article again and complete the sentences.

  1 When you look at career options, you should consider ....

  2 Careers like law or business can give you a ....

  3 For a career in management, you probably need a degree in ....

  4 Some careers don't require a college degree. They require ....

2 Word builder: careers

a Check that you know the meanings of the words in the box. Then write the
occupations in the correct columns in the table.

~~engineer~~   ~~designer~~   veterinarian   ~~social worker~~   ~~accountant~~   animal trainer   salesperson
landscaper   musician   artist   counselor   scientist   doctor   business owner   ~~farmer~~
manager   lawyer   actor   teacher   computer specialist   lab technician

Science / Technology	The Arts	Business / Commerce	Human Services	Agriculture / Nature
engineer	designer	accountant	social worker	farmer

b Try to add at least one more job to each category. Which career area is most
interesting to you? Why? Use ideas from exercise 1 to help.

3 Speaking

a Read the conversations. Do the numbered
sentences express a) agreement,
b) disagreement or c) a reason?

1 – agreement

A: I think people should do jobs
they like.

B: (1) I agree. (2) It's very important
to enjoy your job.

A: I don't think money is
very important.

B: (3) I don't agree. (4) You have to
support your family.

A: You need to have a college degree
to get a good job.

B: (5) You're right.

C: (6) Not necessarily. For some jobs
you only need technical training.

b In groups, discuss the following statements.

1 I think people should do jobs they like.
2 I don't think money is very important.
3 You need to have a college degree to
get a good job.

Unit 8 On the move

1 Getting around

1 Reading

a Scan the text quickly. Look at the photographs below. Match the people with the types of transportation they invented.

b Scan the brochure extract again and check your answers.

A BRIEF HISTORY OF TRANSPORTATION

For centuries people used animals or carriages to move around, but the Industrial Revolution in the 19th century brought the development of new forms of transportation.

In 1829 the first passenger train, built by George Stephenson, started to operate in England. Passengers sat in open carriages, so it was noisy, cold and dirty!

Isambard Kingdom Brunel from England built three ships during his career. In 1838, he built a paddle-steamer which was the first transatlantic passenger steamship. Of course, it was much slower and more uncomfortable than today's luxury cruise liners!

The first powered airplane flight was in 1903 in a plane constructed by the Wright Brothers. However, this flight was not officially documented, and a Brazilian, Santos Dumont, received credit for the first documented flight. His flight was in France in 1906. These early planes were, of course, relatively slow and limited in range.

Karl Benz built the first gasoline-powered automobiles in Germany in 1886, but they were unreliable and often had mechanical problems. In Britain, in 1903, automobiles reached a top speed of 32 km. per hour!

1

The Wright Brothers

2

Benz

3

Brunel

4

Stephenson

A

Passenger train, invented in 1829 by
_____

B

Steamship, invented in 1838 by
_____

C

First powered airplane, invented in 1903 by
_____

D

Gasoline automobile, invented in 1886 by
_____

c   Read the brochure extract again and complete this table.

Type of transportation	Name of inventor(s)	Early disadvantages
1 passenger train		
2		slow and uncomfortable
3		
4	Wright Brothers / Santos Dumont	

2 Speaking and listening

a   Work in pairs. Check that you understand these statements. Decide which of the statements you associate with the forms of transportation in the box.

1 It's expensive.
2 The food isn't good.
3 It's uncomfortable.
4 There are often delays.

5 There's sometimes overbooking.
6 It's tiring.
7 There aren't enough destinations.
8 It's too slow.

bus	train
plane	car

b   Listen to a travel journalist reporting from Chicago's O'Hare airport on forms of transportation. Which is her favorite?

c   Listen again. In her opinion, what are the problems with each form of transportation? Write the numbers from the list in exercise a.
Do you agree with her?

Bus: ..3., 6.
Car: ....
Plane: ....
Train: ....

3 Speaking and writing

a   In pairs, talk about travel in your country. Write a short report answering these questions.

1 What are the most common forms of transportation?
2 What is good and bad about each?
3 What form of transportation do you prefer? Why?

In our country, the most common forms of transportation are …
There are advantages and disadvantages to all these forms of
transportation. For example, …
In our opinion, the best form of transportation is … because …

b   Read your report to another pair. Compare your report with theirs. Do you agree with their opinions?

2 Getting away from it all

1 Speaking and listening

a Look at the picture and answer these questions.

1 Why are the people in the picture using the Internet?

2 What is the relationship between the two people?

b Listen to the conversation and check your answers.

c Read the web page. What kinds of information does it give?

d Now listen to the conversation again and complete the web page.

Address: @ http://www.ontheinternet.com			go ▶
Weekends away	**Lancaster Hotel in Walton**	**Freemont Hotel in Newbridge**	**Beverly Hotel in Southport**
No. of rooms	(1) _____	85	56
Cost of single room per night	(2) _____	(3) _____	$105
Facilities	Gym, squash courts	Sports center, gym, indoor (4)_____ , tennis courts	Fitness center (5) _____
Attractions in the area	Nature Park – a great day outdoors	Colonial Homes Tour – the best preserved 17th century homes in the state	Alton Amusement Park – excitement and the best rides!

(Favorites / History / Search tabs on left side)

2 Grammar builder: superlatives

a Look at these examples. Think about the grammar. Then write the adjectives from the box in the correct columns in the table.

*It's **the biggest** hotel, and it has **the nicest** rooms.* (one-syllable adjectives)

*The Freemont is **the most expensive** hotel.* (multi-syllable adjectives)

*The Freemont is pretty; in fact, it's **the prettiest** hotel.* (adjectives ending in -y)

Irregular adjectives: *good – better – the best   bad – worse – the worst*

One-syllable adjectives	Multi-syllable adjectives	Adjectives ending in -y
the smallest	the most comfortable	the dirtiest

~~dirty~~ famous ~~small~~
historical old cheap
~~comfortable~~ attractive
friendly cold hot
important wonderful
happy clean heavy

b Complete these sentences with superlative forms of adjectives from the box in exercise a. There is more than one possible answer for each sentence.

1 This is .... office in the building.

2 I think cars are .... way to travel.

3 Sam is .... person I know.

4 Jane and Sue are .... people in my office.

3 Reading and speaking

a Look at these titles and read the tourist brochure quickly. Choose the best title.

a) A short history of Colombia

b) A quick guide to vacations in Colombia

c) A guide to Colombian architecture

b Read the tourist brochure again. Which city would you prefer to go to? Why?

BOGOTÁ

The capital and biggest city in Colombia. Very cosmopolitan, great shopping. Don't miss the colonial Candelaria area or the incredible Gold Museum with the largest collection of pre-Columbian gold in the world.

CALI

The most fun city in Colombia! Enjoy outdoor activities all day and dancing to excellent salsa all night. And Cali is famous for having some of the most attractive people in the world! It also has some beautiful architecture.

CARTAGENA

Historically one of the most important Colombian cities. Enjoy some of the best food and most beautiful beaches in the world.

4 Writing and speaking

a In pairs, write tourist information about two places in your country.

b Put the paragraphs on the wall. Read them. Based on the information given, which place would you like to visit and why?

3 Getting there

1 Listening and reading

a Listen to two people talking and answer these questions.

1 Where are these two people?
2 Where are they going?

b Listen to the conversation again and mark the sentences T (true) or F (false).

1 Emilio is Venezuelan.   T ◯   F ◯
2 Marsha is from Miami.   T ◯   F ◯
3 Emilio went to Venezuela to see his family.   T ◯   F ◯
4 Marsha doesn't like Miami very much.   T ◯   F ◯

c Read and complete Emilio's customs declaration. Use the information in the pictures to help you.

CUSTOMS DECLARATION

Admission Number   *Welcome to the United States*

077097360 07

1-94
Arrival Record

1. Family (Last) Name(s) **(1)**

2. First (Given) Name **(2)**

3. Middle Initial(s) **(3)**

4. Birth Date **(4)**

5. Airline Flight No. **(5)**

6. Number of Family Members traveling with you: **(6)**   *0*

7. (a) Country of Citizenship **(7)**

7. (b) Country of Residence **(8)**

8. (a) U.S. Address (Street) **(9)**

8. (b) U.S. Address (City) **(10)**

8. (c) U.S. Address (State) **(11)**

9. Countries visited on this trip prior to U.S. arrival: **(12)**   *VENEZUELA*

10. The purpose of my (our) trip is or was: **(13)** Business   Personal

11. I am (we are) bringing fruits, plants, meats, food, soil, birds, snails, other live animals, wildlife products, farm products;   Yes   No

Airline: American Airlines

Destination: Miami, Florida
Flight no.   AA 564
Name: Emilio Martin Valdez

PASSPORT

PASSPORT NO. 167200675
Family (Last) Name
Martin Valdez
First (Given) Name
Emilio
Nationality
Venezuelan Citizen
Date of birth
04/24/79

VENEZUELA

― *State issued: Miami, Florida* ―
LICENCE NUMBER
ID 276 502 982
DOB 04/24/79
Surname: Martin Valdez
First name: Emilio
Address: 56 Acacia Boulevard, Dale County, Miami, Florida.

Sex: M   Eyes: brown   Ht: 5-09
Issued: 04-12-99   Expires: 05-29-04

Florida DRIVER LICENSE

Emilio Martin Valdez

SAFE DRIVER

2 Grammar builder: *too / either*

a Look at the examples of *too* and *either*. Circle the correct answers for the sentences below.

> A: *I always forget my pens on trips.*
> B: **I do too**! *You know, I don't understand all these forms.*
> A: **I don't either** *and I'm American!*

1 *Too* and *either* express

   a) agreement **b)** disagreement.

2 *Too* is used in

   a) affirmative sentences **b)** negative sentences.

3 *Either* is used in

   a) affirmative sentences **b)** negative sentences.

4 *Too* and *either* are used

   a) before the verb **b)** after the verb.

b Read these sentences and write responses to show agreement.

I'm not hungry. *I'm not either.*

1 I can't ride a motorcycle.
2 I think traveling by bus is very tiring.
3 I don't like the food they serve on planes.
4 I always read when I'm on a train or bus.
5 I hate driving at night.

3 Pronunciation: sentence stress

a Listen and notice the stress in these examples. Practice them.

b Listen to the sentences. Respond to show agreement.

4 Writing and speaking

a Write four sentences about yourself, two affirmative and two negative.

I love sunbathing.

I can't ski.

b In groups, talk about the sentences.

> A: *I love sunbathing.*
> B: *I do too.*
> C: *Really? I don't.*

4 Lifeline to exploration

1 Speaking

a In pairs, match the explorers with the areas of exploration.

1	Marco Polo	**a)**	America
2	Christopher Columbus	**b)**	The undersea world
3	Roald Amundsen	**c)**	China
4	Robert Byrd	**d)**	The South Pole
5	Jacques-Yves Cousteau	**e)**	The moon
6	Neil Armstrong	**f)**	The North Pole

b What else do you know about the explorers above? In groups, discuss these questions.

1 What were their nationalities?

2 When did they live?

3 When did they make their explorations?

4 In your opinion, which two explorations were the most important?

2 Reading

a Read and answer this quiz about the first moon landing. Then compare your answers with a partner.

1 When was the moon landing?

a) 1963 **b)** 1969 **c)** 1971

2 What was the name of the spacecraft?

a) Apollo 11 **b)** Sputnik **c)** Voyager

3 How many astronauts were there?

a) two **b)** three **c)** four

4 Where was the space ship launched?

a) from Texas **b)** from Florida **c)** from California

5 How many astronauts walked on the moon?

a) one **b)** two **c)** three

6 How many days were the astronauts in space?

a) four **b)** eight **c)** ten

b Now read and check your answers to the quiz. Who had more correct answers, you or your partner?

FIRST MAN ON THE MOON

July 20, 1969 was one of the most important days in the history of the United States and of the world. On that day, two U.S. astronauts walked on the surface of the moon!

The journey of the spacecraft Apollo 11 began on July 16, when it took off from Cape Kennedy in Florida. There were three specially trained astronauts on the ship – Neil Armstrong, Edwin Aldrin and Michael Collins. The spacecraft carried several tons of equipment, including oxygen tanks, special space suits and a moon vehicle.

At exactly 10:56 Florida time, Neil Armstrong became the first person to step onto the moon! The words he spoke at that moment became famous: "That's one small step for a man, one giant leap for mankind." He and Edwin Aldrin spent two hours on the lunar surface while Michael Collins stayed in the spacecraft.

On July 24, Apollo 11 returned safely to earth. The three astronauts were home and they were international heroes.

3 Listening

a Listen to the interview. What type of exploration is the subject of the conversation?

a) exploration of the Poles **b)** undersea exploration **c)** space exploration

b Listen again and check (✓) the problems the expert mentions.

○ fatigue   ○ no natural oxygen   ○ extreme temperatures
○ bad food   ○ uncomfortable conditions ○ gravity differences

4 Writing and speaking

a In groups, discuss these questions.

1 What explorers are associated with your country or area of the world?

2 What did they do?

b Look at this paragraph about Christopher Columbus. Rewrite it about another explorer by changing the underlined information.

Christopher Columbus was an Italian explorer in the 15th century. In 1492, he began his most famous journey in Spain. He traveled by ship. During his journey, he discovered America. He claimed the New World for Spain. I think the problems on his journey were probably fatigue, bad food, uncomfortable conditions and bad weather.

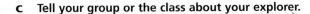

c Tell your group or the class about your explorer.

Checkpoint 4

1 Check your progress

a Read and complete the conversation.

Jerry: I really want to go to the beach.

Ruth: I (**1**)........................ . But let's find a small hotel. I don't like big modern hotels.

Jerry: I don't (**2**)........................ . OK. A small hotel on the beach. But where?

Travel agent: Hmm. Florida has wonderful beaches.

Ruth: We (**3**)........................ (*go*) to Florida two years ago. I prefer somewhere different.

Jerry: I (**4**)........................ too. Look. What about Venezuela?

Travel agent: Well, it's (**5**)........................ (*old*) but (**6**) it's .... (*expensive*) than Florida. It's a beautiful place for a vacation.

Ruth: I think it's a great idea.

Jerry: Hm … Puerto Angel. The beaches look (**7**)........................ (*good*) than Florida.

Ruth: And we can visit Angel Falls. They're (**8**)........................ (*high*) falls in the world!

b Complete their postcard with the correct form of the words in parentheses.

Hi everyone,

We (9) _____ (*arrive*) in Venezuela last Saturday and (10) _____ (*spend*) two very nice days in Caracas. We (11) _____ (*go*) to a lovely area called "Haltillo." It's the (12) _____ (*old*) part of the city. We (13) _____ (*buy*) lots of presents in the market. The city is quite high so it's (14) _____ (*cool*) than the coastal areas.

Yesterday evening we (15) _____ (*eat*) arepas – delicious corn cakes. Very tasty. We (16) _____ (*fly*) to Puerto Angel this morning and the flight only (17) _____ (*take*) 30 minutes. Puerto Angel is much, much (18) _____ (*small*) than Caracas.

Next Thursday we (19) _____ (*travel*) to Angel Falls. After that, we (20) _____ (*go*) to Merida – an old colonial city. See you soon!

Love,

Ruth and Jerry

Score out of 20

○ 18–20 Excellent! ○ 15–17 Very good! ○ 12–14 OK, but review. ○ 9–11 You have some problems. Review units 7 and 8. ○ 0–8 Talk to your teacher.

76

2 Games to play

a Work in groups. Choose a pair of topics from 1–4 and make as many comparative sentences as possible. The group with the most correct sentences wins.

Dogs / cats: *Dogs are bigger than cats. Cats are quieter than dogs. Dogs are friendlier than cats*, etc.

1 A BMW / a Volkswagen beetle
2 Dolphins / sharks
3 Japanese food / Italian food
4 A city / a small town

b Work in groups. Look at the four situations below. Make a request for each situation and invent a reason to persuade your group. The group decides which request is the best.

Can I borrow your bike? I have to take this video back or pay a $25 fine!

1 You want someone to lend you $50.00.
2 You want someone to give you a ride to the bus station.
3 You want someone to take care of your cat while you go on vacation.
4 You would like someone to lend you his / her laptop so you can finish a report.

3 Your world

a In pairs, write down these facts for your country.

1 The biggest city
2 The highest mountain
3 The longest river
4 The most popular vacation resort
5 The most beautiful part of the country
6 The most typical food and drink
7 The most famous singer
8 The official language(s)
9 The name of the money
10 The most common names for men and women

b Compare your answers with another pair. Ask questions to check your answers.

What's the longest river?

4 Personal word bank

Add more words that are important to you. Compare your lists with a partner.

School: subjects / people	Jobs	Transportation	Phrases
math	accountant	plane	Could you lend me #5.00?
principal	social worker		

Unit 9 Healthy living

1 Laughter is the best medicine

1 Speaking and listening

a In pairs, choose four things from the list which you think affect health the most. Then compare your list with another pair.

Early signs of a heart attack

1	character	4	exercise	7	hours of sleep
2	diet	5	family environment	8	relaxation and fun
3	job	6	family medical history	9	habits: smoking, drinking, etc.

b Listen to a doctor's opinions on health. Which things does he consider most important?

c Listen again. Then complete this table with the doctor's recommendations.

Do	Don't
1 have a good diet – lot of fruits and vegetables	1
2	2
3	3 go to bed late too often
4	4

2 Speaking and reading

a Read the article. What are the two main reason young people in
Europe are not very healthy?

An unhealthy lifestyle

Your lifestyle can influence your health. Young Europeans today are less healthy than their parents and grandparents because of their lifestyle. Research shows that about 15% of European adults are overweight, compared with about one in five of European young people. There are two main reasons for this.

First, junk food and unhealthy fast food are everywhere. A lot of mothers and fathers are working and fast food is the easiest way to solve the problem of meals for their children. Also, the fast food industry spends 1,000 times more on marketing and advertising in Europe and the U.S. than the total amount spent by all agencies on promoting health in the two regions!

Second, computers and television keep children sedentary for longer periods than ever before. And many parents are worried about crime so they don't let their children play outside or ride their bicycles to school. These changes in lifestyle could create major future health problems for Europeans.

b In groups, look at these statements and say if they are true
for your country.

1 People eat a lot of fast food and junk food.

2 People don't get enough exercise.

3 Life is more stressful than in the past.

4 Many people work very long hours.

c Suggest ways to deal with the problems in exercise b.

3 Reading and speaking

a Read this fitness quiz and answer the questions. How fit are you?

Measure your fitness

1 *How much do you exercise?*
   a) once a week ☐   b) 2–3 times a week ☐   c) every day ☐

2 *How often do you eat fresh fruit and vegetables?*
   a) 1–2 times a week ☐   b) 3–4 times a week ☐   c) every day ☐

3 *How many cups of coffee or colas do you drink per day?*
   a) 4 or more ☐   b) 2–3 ☐   c) 0–1 ☐

4 *How many hours do you sleep at night?*
   a) 5 or fewer ☐   b) about 6 ☐   c) 7–9 ☐

5 *How often do you eat cookies and chocolate?*
   a) every day ☐   b) 3–4 times a week ☐   c) 0–2 times a week ☐

6 *How much TV do you watch per week?*
   a) 28 hours or more ☐   b) 14–20 hours ☐   c) 10 hours or less ☐

a = 0 points
b = 1 point
c = 2 points

10–12: Congratulations! You're super fit!

6–9: Not too bad, but do more exercise and watch your diet.

0–5: Oh dear! You're very unfit! You need to eat better and exercise more! Now!

b Compare your scores with another student. Do you have any advice for your
partner?

2 Your favorite team

1 Word builder: sports and exercise

a Write the words in the box in the correct column. Can you think of another word for each column?

Play	Go	Do

jogging   windsurfing   karate   hiking
rugby   soccer   aerobics   exercises
riding (a bicycle or horseback)   basketball
tae-kwon-do   tennis

b Complete the sentences with a verb from the box.

1 We use .... when we think of the sport as an activity, like swimming.
2 We use .... for exercise in general, and for martial arts, like karate.
3 We use .... for games, like volleyball.

play   go   do

c In pairs, discuss the questions.

1 Which sports do you like watching?   2 Which ones do you like doing?

2 Grammar builder: possessive pronouns

Look at the rule and the examples. Then complete the cartoon with possessive pronouns.

Use possessive pronouns to avoid repetition.

*That car is my car. = That car is **mine**.*
*Those shoes are Linda's shoes. = Those shoes are **hers**.*
*These shirts are the boys' shirts. = These shirts are **theirs**.*

mine	ours
yours	yours
his	theirs
hers	

"No, it isn't (2) _____.
It's (3) _____."

"No, it isn't. It's
(4) _____."

"No, it's
(5) _____."

"Is this baseball
(1) _____?"

"It isn't
(6) _____!"

"Well then, you can all pay for my window!"

3 Listening and reading

a Listen to a conversation and answer the questions.

1 Where are they?   2 What is Manchester United?

b Listen again and complete this information.

Manchester United – vital statistics

Colors (1) ....

Year founded (2) ....

Year of first championship (3) ....

Capacity of stadium (4) ....

Where they get money: stockmarket shares, sports

products, (5) .... , (6) ....

and a TV company.

c Now read this article and check your answers.

A GAME OR A BUSINESS?

Manchester United Football Club (Manchester, England) was founded in 1878, and they won their first championship in 1907. Today, they are one of the best soccer teams in the world, and thousands of fans go to their games. Their home stadium, Old Trafford, was built in 1910, with a capacity of 50,000 people. Today the stadium has a capacity of 68,000.

Manchester United is also the richest soccer team in the world. The "Red Devils" (whose team colors are red and white) receive 176 million dollars per year – 48 million more than Spain's Real Madrid!

Where does so much money come from? Manchester United is a Public Limited Company, with shares on the stockmarket. The team has a store which sells sports products, and it also owns a hotel, several restaurants (all called the Red Café) and a TV company. The team's directors would probably say that diversity is the name of the game – but is it a game, or just another big business?

4 Speaking

In groups, discuss these questions.

1 What are the most important sports in your country?

2 Who are your favorite teams and players?

3 Are the sports big business? If so, where do they get their money?

4 In your opinion, how could they make more money?

3 Open wide

1 Listening

a The words in the box are all related to dental health. Look up new words in your dictionary.

teeth	toothbrush	dentist	floss
filling	cavity	gums	toothpaste

b Listen to part A of a telephone conversation between a dentist and a patient. What is the problem?

c Now listen to part B of the conversation and check (✓) the advice you hear.

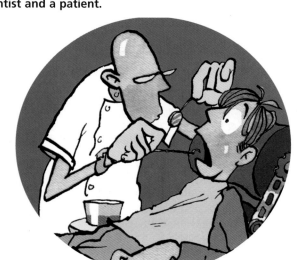

- ◯ 1 Brush your teeth at least twice a day.
- ◯ 2 Brush your teeth after meals.
- ◯ 3 You should use mouthwash.
- ◯ 4 Floss your teeth.
- ◯ 5 Don't drink coffee.
- ◯ 6 You should brush your teeth for three minutes.
- ◯ 7 You shouldn't change your toothbrush often.
- ◯ 8 You should go to the dentist every six months.

2 Pronunciation: sounds - /ɪ/ and /i/

a Write the words in the box in the correct column in the table according to the sounds.

/ɪ/	/i/
if	see

live	see	eat	fill	sit
she	it	three	if	teeth

b Listen, check and practice the words.

3 Reading

a Look at the titles. Read the poster on page 83 quickly and choose the best title.

   a) Taking care of your teeth   **b)** A history of dental care   **c)** Diet and your teeth

b Read the poster again. Match the spaces with the advice in exercise 1c.

TEETH

Did you know that people a long time ago cleaned their teeth with chalk, lemon juice, ashes or tobacco and honey? Toothpaste was invented only about 100 years ago, and brushing teeth only became popular during World War II.

You have to take care of your teeth all your life. To keep them healthy, you need to brush them at least (a) ___1___, after breakfast and before bed. Brushing after lunch or after sweet snacks is a good idea. You should brush your teeth for at least (b) _____ .

Make sure you change your toothbrush every three months. You should (c) _____ your teeth. This removes food that your toothbrush can't reach. You should also use (d) _____ to help keep your breath fresh.

It's also important to visit the dentist (e) _____ . The dentist checks for cavities and gum disease and helps you keep your teeth extra clean.

Finally, you need to be careful about what you eat and drink. Eat lots of fruit and vegetables and drink milk or water instead of soda.

4 Grammar builder: *should / need to / have to*

a **Read these sentences and underline the words which give advice. Which sentence is "the strongest?"**

1 You have to take care of your teeth all your life.

2 To keep your teeth healthy, you need to brush them at least twice a day.

3 You should brush your teeth for at least three minutes.

b **Find and correct the error in each of these sentences.**

1 You should to eat healthy foods.

2 I need go to the dentist because I have a toothache.

3 We have to exercising every day to stay healthy.

5 Writing and speaking

a **Choose one of the problems from this list and write two sentences giving advice. Use *You should / need to / have to ...***

1 I often have headaches.

2 I feel very stressed.

3 I need to lose weight.

4 I'm tired all the time.

5 I feel bored with my life!

6 I have a toothache.

b **In groups, read your advice. Can your group guess the problem?**

4 Lifeline to living things

1 Reading and speaking

a How much do you know about hair? Read the quiz and answer the questions.

b Compare your answers with a partner. Then read the text to check your answers. Who knows more about hair – you or your partner?

QUIZ

1 **What is the purpose of hair?**
   a) to warm and protect the body ○   b) to keep the skin clean ○
   c) to make people attractive to other people ○

2 **About how many hairs are on the human head?**
   a) 20,000 ○   b) 50,000 ○   c) 100,000 ○

3 **For how many years does each hair grow?**
   a) 1–2 ○   b) 3–4 ○   c) 5–6 ○

4 **About how long can each hair grow?**
   a) 60 centimeters ○   b) 1 meter ○   c) 1.5 meters ○

5 **About how much does hair grow every month?**
   a) ½ centimeter ○   b) 1 centimeter ○   c) 2 centimeters ○

6 **What determines hair type and color?**
   a) hair follicles and melanin ○   b) diet when you're a baby ○
   c) exposure to sun when you're a baby ○

Hair everywhere

Hair covers almost every part of your body. The only parts of the body that do not have hair are the lips, the palms of the hands and soles of the feet. Hair keeps you warm and gives your body some protection.

You have over 100,000 hairs on your head. Each hair grows for about 5 to 6 years. If hair is not cut, it can grow up to 1.5 meters long! Hair grows very slowly – about 1 centimeter a month. It also falls out, and you lose about 50 to 100 hairs every day. When a hair finishes growing, it falls out and a new hair grows in its place.

The type and color of your hair depend on two things: hair follicles and melanin. If you have large hair follicles, your hair will be thick. If your follicles are small, your hair will be fine. The structure of the follicles determines if you have straight, curly or wavy hair. Hair color comes from melanin. More melanin means darker hair, less melanin means lighter hair. Skin color often goes with hair color: many blonds have light skin, while people with darker skin usually have dark brown or black hair.

2 Speaking

In groups, say whether you agree or disagree with these statements about hair.

1 I don't care what my hair looks like. It isn't important.
2 I never want to have gray hair. I don't want to look old!
3 Men with long hair don't look professional.
4 People's hairstyle usually reflects their personality.
5 I'm worried that I'll be bald when I'm older!

3 Writing and speaking

a Look at the examples. Choose one of the photos on these two pages and write a description of the person. Include as many details as possible.

brown eyes

dark skin

long, wavy brown hair

dark brown beard

brown mustache

long, straight blond hair

blue eyes

light skin

b In groups, read your description. Your classmates try to guess which photograph you are describing.

Unit 10 The story so far

1 Turning points

1 Speaking and reading

a Look at the photographs. What do you know about these people?

b Read this article and complete the star profile.

Love of the Game

André Agassi is a hometown boy. He was born in Las Vegas, and he has always lived there. However, he has been around the world many times. And he has made more than $20 million. As a tennis professional, he has won the Wimbledon, French, U.S. and Australian Open Tennis Championships – "Grand Slam" titles.

André was born in 1970, became a professional in 1986, made his first million dollars in 1990, and won his first Grand Slam title in 1992 – Wimbledon. He won more than $2 million in 1994 and almost $3 million in 1995. He ended both years ranked Number 2.

He began dating Brooke Shields, beautiful teenage star of the 1980 hit movie *Blue Lagoon*. Life was good, but his tennis was not so good. He fell to Number 8 in the 1996 rankings, and then to Number 110 in 1997, the year he and Brooke got married.

The turning point in his life was in 1999. He and Brooke separated and then divorced. And in that same year he won the French, Wimbledon and U.S. Opens, rose to Number 1 ranking, and made more than $4 million.

Star Profile

Name: **(1)** _____

Hometown: **(2)** _____

Year of birth: **(3)** _____

Became professional: **(4)** _____

First Grand Slam title: **(5)** _____,19____

Ranking in 1994/5: **(6)** _____

Year of marriage: **(7)** _____

Ranking in 1996: **(8)** _____

Year of divorce: **(9)** _____

1999 statistics:

Major tennis titles: **(10)** _____

_____

Ranking: **(11)** _____

Income: **(12)** _____

c In groups, discuss these questions.

1 In your opinion, what were the turning points in Agassi's life?

2 Do you know of another famous person with good and bad years?

2 Speaking and listening

a Write the title of each movie and the name of the actress who appeared in it under each photograph.

A *Title of movie:*

....

Actress: ....

B *Title of movie:*

....

Actress: ....

C *Title of movie:*

....

Actress: ....

b In groups, check your answers.

c Listen to a conversation about one of the actresses. Who is it?

d Listen again. Match each of these events in her life to a movie.

1 Her first big opportunity.

2 She became a popular actor's girlfriend.

3 She won the Oscar for Best Actress.

a) *Shakespeare in Love*

b) *Hook*

c) *Seven*

3 Writing and speaking

a Write sentences about your good and bad years. Don't write your name!

1997 was a bad year for me. I broke my leg, and I failed a course at school.

1999 was a very important year for me. I got a better job, and I met my future husband there.

b In groups, mix up the papers. Someone takes a paper and reads the notes to the group. The group tries to guess the person. Then ask him / her for more information.

Which course did you fail?

How did you break your leg?

2 Experience and experiences

1 Speaking and listening

a In pairs, look at the photograph and try to answer the questions.

1 Where was Angie Li born?
2 Where does she live now?
3 What languages does she speak?

4 What is her job?
5 Are there many women with the same job?
6 What was her most dramatic experience?

b Listen to a radio interview with Angie Li and check your answers to exercise a.

c In groups, discuss these questions.

1 Which jobs in your country are typically for men, and which for women?
2 Is the proportion of men and women in certain jobs changing? Give some examples.

2 Grammar builder: present perfect

a Read the sentences and match them with the uses of the present perfect.

1 **Have** you ever **had** an emergency? Yes, I **have**. Two years ago we landed without wheels.
2 Angie Li works for Western Airlines. She **has** always **work**ed there.
3 André Agassi **has made** more than $20 million, and he will probably make a lot more.

a) an action which happened in the past, and can happen again in the future
b) a question about life experiences
c) an action which began in the past and continues in the present

b Look at the sentences again. How do you express these ideas in your language?

c Look at the example in the table and then complete the sentences with the present perfect. Use the past participles from the box. Then check your answers with a partner.

subject	have / has	past participle	
She	has	been	to Spain three times.

Regular verbs: studied   worked   lived
Irregular verbs: seen   read   done

1 I' .ve.. .... in this town all my life.
2 .... you ever .... for a big company? No, I ....
3 I'...... .... English for two years.
4 Paula .... never .... a Steven Spielberg movie.
5 .... George .... his homework? Yes, he ....
6 .... you ever .... a book by Octavio Paz? No, never.

Language assistant

- *Ever* indicates "at any time in your life until now." It is used in questions.
  Have you ever ...?

- *Never* indicates "at no time in your life."
  I've never had a dog.

3 Speaking

a Answer the questionnaire. Put a check (✓) for Yes and a cross (✗) for No.

Are you an adventurer

... in the world of action?

Have you ever
- climbed a big mountain?
- been hang-gliding?
- swum across a river or lake?
- camped in an isolated place?
- traveled a long distance with little money?

... in the world of the mind?

Have you ever
- been to a symphony concert?
- read a Shakespeare play?
- been to a famous art gallery or museum?
- read a whole science book?
- written a poem or a story?

b Try to find someone who has done each thing. Ask questions beginning *Have you ever ...?* Also ask questions beginning *When ...?*, *Where...?* and *What ...?*

A: Have you ever read a Shakespeare play?   *A: What did you read?*
B: Yes, I have.   *B: I read "Macbeth" at school.*

3 Champions' stories

1 Speaking and reading

a Look at the photograph. Do you like auto racing? Why or why not? Do you know anything about Michael Schumacher?

b Try to answer these questions. Then read the article to check your answers.

1 Who won the 1995 San Marino Grand Prix?

2 Who was 1995 Formula 1 Champion?

3 Between 1996 and 2000, was Schumacher more important for Ferrari, or Ferrari more important for Schumacher?

4 Why didn't Schumacher win the Driver's Championship in 1999?

5 What are Schumacher's three most important qualities as a race car driver?

PAST AND FUTURE CHAMPION

Frank Voltaire, at Imola, San Marino, April 9, 2000

It was a close race here at Imola, but Schumacher beat champion Mika Hakkinen. So Michael Schumacher and Ferrari have won all three Grand Prix so far this year.

When Schumacher moved to Ferrari in 1996, he was the Formula 1 Champion, but Ferrari was losing races. In the four years since then, he has made Ferrari successful. Sadly, he missed the Driver's Championship in 1999 only because of a broken leg.

Schumacher won the Championship twice with Benetton, in 1994 and 1995, and I am sure he will make it three times this year. At 31, he has not finished winning races. His driving ability is evident. He is completely dedicated to auto racing, and he also has more technical knowledge than most race car drivers. There is no doubt that Schumacher is a past and future champion.

2 **Grammar builder:** verb forms

a Write the verbs in the box in the correct columns. Check your answers with a partner.

	break	swim	come
	travel	camp	drink
	climb	study	write
	go	eat	live	fail
	do	win	fall	see
	make	read	work

Regular	Irregular	Regular	Irregular	Regular	Irregular
camp	break				
climb	come				

b In pairs, match the past and past participle forms with the infinitives of the irregular verbs.

Past

read   swam   wrote   ~~broke~~
saw   did   ate   won   drank
made   went   came

Past participle

done   gone   read   won   seen
written   swum   drunk   come
eaten   ~~broken~~   made

Infinitive	Past	Past participle	Infinitive	Past	Past participle
break	broke	broken	drink		
write			swim		
eat			make		
see			read		
go			win		
do			come		

3 **Pronunciation:** sounds – vowels

a Write the verb forms in the box in the correct vowel pronunciation column.

~~ate~~   ~~come~~   read (past)   seen   broken   break   made
~~fell~~   read (present)   went   ~~broke~~   done   make   go
won   eaten   ~~eat~~   drunk   read (past participle)   wrote

see /i/	day /eɪ/	yes /e/	no /oʊ/	cup /ʌ/
eat	ate	fell	broke	come

b Listen, check your answers, and practice pronouncing the verbs.

4 Lifeline to clothes design

1 Word builder: describing clothes

a Match the words and phrases in the box with the photographs.

plain	tight	loose	wide leg
short	long, wide sleeve		patterned

Photograph A: plain, …

b The fashions in the photographs are from the 1940s, 1960s and 1990s. Which of the three periods do you prefer? Are fashions now very different from fashions in the 1990s?

c Describe the clothes of different people in your class.

Carla is wearing loose white pants, a short plain blue top and black boots.

2 Reading and speaking

a Read the list of topics. Then read the article and match the topics with the paragraphs.

1 the development of modern fashion: paragraph ◯
2 fashion and marketing: paragraph ◯
3 fashion isn't just about style – it's also about being practical: paragraph ◯

Fashion designers and marketers

A Modern fashion originated principally in Europe. But the concept of fashion is nothing new. If you look at European paintings of the past thousand or more years you can tell the approximate date of the painting, from the clothes. People in different European countries began to wear the same fashions at the same period. And so a new cosmopolitan career developed: fashion designer.

B It's not only about a "look" though. Fashion takes into account some practical factors. There are winter, spring, summer and fall fashions for the changing climate, and formal, informal and sports fashions for

different activities. But other factors, which have nothing to do with convenience, are also prominent in modern fashion design.

C On one hand, fashion design is considered an art form. For centuries designers have created beautiful or shocking clothes. On the other hand, fashion is the result of modern marketing. Designers work with marketers to stimulate the clothing economy (people buy new clothes because fashions change). Marketers and designers also create new markets such as for older teenagers and young professionals.

b In groups, discuss these questions.

1 What different clothes do you wear at different times of the year and for different activities?

2 What are some of your favorite fashions at the moment?

3 Are there some fashions that you don't like? Why?

3 Reading, speaking and listening

a Read and imagine this situation.

In your hometown there is only one important company, a clothes manufacturer, Nuway Fashion. They are looking for the following staff.

1 A production manager (responsible for the clothes-making equipment and quality control).

2 A designer (capable of creating clothes that will be attractive for young people).

3 A marketing and sales manager (responsible for selling the clothes).

4 A financial manager (responsible for the company's money).

b Listen to a job interview. Which of the jobs does the applicant want?

c Listen again. Write the the applicant's relevant qualifications and experience in the table.

Qualifications	Experience
1	1
	2

4 Writing and speaking

a Imagine you have started to work as a designer for Nuway Fashion. Design an article of clothing. Do a drawing and complete the designer's form.

nf Nuway fashion	DESIGN DETAILS
	Type of clothing
	Season
	Target buyer
	Description

b Put the designs on the wall and vote for the best one.

Checkpoint 5

1 Check your progress

a Complete the conversation with words from the box.

whose	hers	yours	theirs	his	's (x2)	mine

Coach: OK. Let's get organized. (**1**)................ is this red bag?

Ben: Oh, thanks. It's (**2**)................ .

Coach: Here you are. And the blue bag? Is it (**3**)................ , Marsha?

Marsha: No, I think it's Sandra (**4**)................ .

Coach: And this black suitcase. Is it Steve's?

Marsha: Yeah, it's (**5**)................ . It's all dirty!!

Coach: And these magazines?

Sandra: I saw Teresa and Marsha reading them. They're probably (**6**)................ .

Coach: And these candies?

Ben: Hmm. Sandra loves candies so they must be (**7**)................ .

Sandra: No, they aren't. They're Paul (**8**)................ .

b Complete the star profile with the correct form of the verbs in parentheses.

Cameron Díaz (**9**) _____ (be) born in 1972. She's a very successful actress and (**10**) _____ (make) a series of hit movies including *My Best Friend's Wedding* and *There's Something About Mary.*

But acting (**11**) _____ (not be) her first career. She (**12**) _____ (go) to school in California and (**13**) _____ (become) a model when she (**14**) _____ (be) 16 years

old. In 1993, she (**15**) _____ (decide) to be an actress and (**16**) _____ (get) a leading part in *The Mask* with Jim Carrey.

As a model, she (**17**) _____ (travel) all over the world, but she (**18**) _____ (live) in Hollywood for the last eight years. She (**19**) _____ (not win) an Oscar yet, but she (**20**) _____ (achieve) her dream of being a movie star.

Score out of 20

| ● 18–20 Excellent! | ● 15–17 Very good! | ● 12–14 OK, but review. | ● 9–11 You have some problems. Review units 9 and 10. | ● 0–8 Talk to your teacher. |

2 Games to play

a Do this word puzzle to find the mystery word. Then check your answers in pairs or groups.

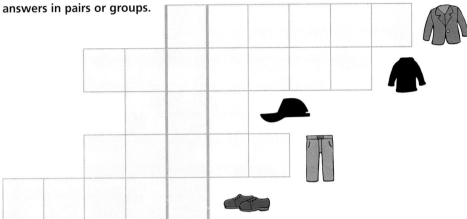

b In pairs, play "word tennis." Choose from these categories: sports, the body, clothes and health. You say a word and your partner says a different word. Continue until one person can't think of any other words in the category. The winner gets one point.

A: teeth   *B: toothpaste*

3 Your world

Complete the table for you. Write Y (Yes) or N (No). Then interview a partner using *Have you ever ...?* to complete the Your partner column. If your partner says "Yes", ask questions to fill in the Details column.

Experience	You Y / N	Your partner Y / N	Details
1 meet someone famous			
2 have an accident			
3 win a prize			
4 stay up all night			
5 do bungee jumping			
6 have an unusual pet			

4 Personal word bank

Add more words that are important to you. Compare your lists with a partner.

Keeping fit	Sports	Irregular verbs			Phrases
unfit	tennis championship	fall	fell	fallen	Have you ever climbed a mountain?

Unit 11 Ways of life

1 Traditions

1 Speaking and listening

a Look at the photographs. In pairs, discuss these questions.

   1 What are the different traditions?

   2 Which countries do you associate the traditions with?

b Listen to an interview with three young people. Write Y (Yes) in the table if they like traditional things or modern things and N (No) if they don't like them.

	Likes traditional things	Likes modern things
First person		
Second person		
Third person		

2 Speaking and reading

a In groups, discuss what you know about the Rio de Janeiro carnival. Talk about these things.

   1 Time of year   3 Traditional dance and music

   2 Length of celebration   4 Kinds of costumes

b Do you have a festival like the Rio carnival in your country?

c Read the article about the Quebec carnival. Answer these questions in pairs.

1 What carnivals has the writer been to?

2 What is the main difference between the Quebec carnival and most other traditional carnivals?

3 What different events are there at the Quebec carnival?

4 How do people keep warm during the outdoor events?

5 What is it important to do if you want to attend the carnival, especially the last Saturday?

6 Would you like to attend the Quebec carnival? Why or why not?

Cool carnival

I used to associate carnival with the warm south – New Orleans, Mazatlán, Veracruz, Bahía, and Rio de Janeiro. I love carnivals, and I've been to all those traditional ones. But last year I did something very different – I went north, to Quebec, where the French Canadians have celebrated carnival for more than 100 years.

February is a cold, cold month in Quebec. Ice and snow are usually a problem in the long Canadian winter, but at carnival they are two of the main ingredients of the festivities. In the park across from the National Assembly they make an enormous Ice Palace, and fantastic human and animal figures from ice and snow.

You need action to keep warm in that climate, and there's lots of that. There are ice hockey games, races on the ice, dances, and of course, parades. The musicians wrap up their instruments so they don't freeze. So you don't freeze, you can follow the parade, or you can drink "Cariboo," made from red wine and whiskey – or you can do both things, and completely forget the cold!

The most spectacular event is the Night Parade on the last Saturday. Crowds of tourists come to see it. The hotels are always full, so make your reservations in advance.

3 Word builder: *do / make*

a Look at the rules for the use of *do* and *make* and then complete the sentences with the correct forms of *do* and *make*.

a) We normally use *do* for actions, activities, work, etc.

 *We **do** a job.*

b) We normally use *make* for products, constructions, results, etc.

 *We **make** a mess.*

1 Last year the writer .... something different. He went to Quebec.

2 They .... an enormous Ice Palace in the park.

3 You need to .... some exercise to keep warm.

4 They .... "Cariboo" out of red wine and whiskey.

5 The hotels .... a lot of money during carnival.

6 The carnival committee .... a lot of work before the event.

> **Language assistant**
>
> In English we do not *do / make* a question; we *ask* a question.

b In groups, talk about things you've done or made recently.

I've made plans for this Friday. I'm going dancing with some friends.

2 Your life

1 Reading and speaking

a **Read and complete the paragraph.**

I'm 25 years (1)………. . I live alone in a small apartment in Detroit. I moved to Detroit from my family home in New Jersey (2)………1999. My family (3)……… always lived in New Jersey. I'm (4)……… engineer, and I work in an automobile plant. I began working there (5)……… 2000. My main hobby is karate. I began when I (6)……… 12 years old, and I'm really good now – a black belt. I also started studying Spanish two years ago because my last boyfriend was Cuban. I don't (7)……… a boyfriend now, but I want (8)……… continue studying Spanish. I'm looking for a private teacher.

b **Check your answers with a partner.**

2 Listening

a **Listen to Joanna's telephone conversation. Who is she talking to?**

b **Listen again then complete these sentences about Ana.**

1 Ana Vieira was born in

……………… .

2 She is ……………… years old.

3 She has lived in the U.S. for ……………… years.

4 She has lived in Detroit since ……………… of last year.

5 She has taught Spanish and Portuguese since

……………… .

6 She has given classes at a language institute for ……………… months.

3 Grammar builder: present perfect with *for* / *since* and *How long?*

a Look at the two boxes. Which phrases refer to a point in time and which to a period of time? Match the boxes with these incomplete sentences.

1 They have been here since …

2 They have been here for …

A	B
… four years	… 1998
… six months	… last July
… two hours	… Monday
… twenty minutes	… three o'clock

b Complete this conversation with information about Joanna Long. Look at exercise 1a for help.

Ana: Are you originally from Detroit, Joanna?

Joanna: No, I'm from ....

Ana: How long have you lived here?

Joanna: Since ....

Ana: And how long have you studied Spanish?

Joanna: For ....

Ana: Have you ever studied another language?

Joanna: No, ...

4 Pronunciation: stress and rhythm

Listen and underline the stressed words in these sentences. Notice the contractions – *'ve* for *have* and the weak form of *you*. Practice the questions and answers in pairs.

1 How long have you lived here?

2 I've lived here since 1999.

3 How long have you studied Spanish?

4 I've studied it for two years.

5 Speaking

a Find out the following information about people in your class.

Who	How long has he / she
plays a musical instrument?	played the instrument?
has a computer at home?	had the computer?
is engaged or married?	been engaged or married?
plays on a sports team?	played on the team?

A: *Do you play a musical instrument?*

B: *Yes, I play the guitar.*

A: *How long have you played it?*

B: *Oh … for a long time. Since elementary school.*

b In groups, talk about the information.

David plays the guitar. He's played it for many years, since elementary school.

Language assistant

Note the contraction for *He* / *She* / *It has* – *He's* / *She's* / *It's.*

3 Working together

1 Reading and speaking

a Look at the two photographs and talk about the differences.

b Look at these topics. Read the article quickly. Match the topics with the paragraphs.

1 recent changes in some institutional cultures: paragraph ◯

2 an institution that always has a very hierarchical culture: paragraph ◯

3 the cultures of many traditional institutions: paragraph ◯

Institutional cultures

A Certain institutions always have strongly hierarchical cultures. An army is a perfect example. Uniforms indicate rank. Officers are addressed as "Sir" or with a title – Major, Captain, etc. When superiors tell subordinates to do things, these orders cannot be questioned. The principle behind all this is that, in life-or-death situations, discipline and instant action are more important than democratic discussion.

B Most institutions used to have similar hierarchical cultures, and many still do. In "traditional" schools, children stand up when teachers enter, address them as "Sir" or "Miss," and raise a hand for permission to speak. Employees in many schools, companies and government offices also behave in this way with their bosses.

C But things have changed in many places. In modern schools, students often address teachers by their first names, and there is a lot of open discussion in class. In the business world, companies like Microsoft became famous for informal dress, and "democratic" management. This was because these companies wanted everyone to think critically and creatively.

---

c Read the article again. Answer these questions.

1 Which institution is a clear example of a hierarchical culture?

2 Why is discipline so important in an army?

3 How do children behave in "traditional" schools?

4 How do children in "modern" schools often address the teachers?

5 What aspects of Microsoft's corporate culture became famous?

d In groups, discuss these questions.

1 How formal or informal was / is your school / college / workplace?

2 Are levels of formality changing? If yes, do you agree with the changes? If no, do you think they should change?

2 Grammar builder: *tell / ask / want*

a **Look at these sentences. How would you express these ideas in your language?**

1 Superiors tell subordinates to do things.
2 The company wanted everyone to think critically and creatively.
3 The teacher told the students to pay attention.
4 He told them not to play in class.
5 The manager asked the secretaries not to make personal telephone calls without permission.

b **Look at the cartoon and complete these sentences.**

1 The officer asked Smith .... a shave.
2 He told Brown ....
3 He told Hill ....
4 He told them ....
5 He wants them ....

> ### Language assistant
>
> - Use *ask* instead of *tell* to indicate politeness.
>   *She asked me not to smoke.*
>
> - Use *tell* for orders and for giving information.
>   *She told me not to smoke.*
>   *He told me the news.*
>
> - You can use *not to* after *tell / ask*, but not after *want*. Compare:
>   *He told me not to smoke.*
>   *He didn't want me to smoke.*

Smith, could you please shave?

Brown, cut your hair!

Hill, don't wear any rings in your nose!

Don't smoke on parade!

They have to look good for the general tomorrow.

3 Writing and speaking

a **Write a sentence for each of these situations.**

1 something your parents always told you to do
2 something they told you not to do
3 something you want your children to do
4 something you don't want them to do

My parents always told me to …
They told me not to …

b **In groups, compare your ideas.**

4 Lifeline to business administration

1 Word builder: business vocabulary

These words are all related to international business. How many of them do you know? With a partner, match the words with their definitions.

1	investment	**a)**	work, jobs
2	employment	**b)**	money paid for work
3	wages	**c)**	the process of designing or creating something
4	manufacturing	**d)**	investigation, especially scientific
5	research	**e)**	production process
6	development	**f)**	money put into a bank or a business to make more money

2 Speaking and reading

a Look at these titles. Read the magazine article and choose the best title.

   a) Everything will soon be multinational

   b) Multinationals have a permanent place

   c) The end of multinationals is near

MULTINATIONALS have a mixed reputation. On one hand, they provide investment and employment around the world, which is especially important in poorer countries. On the other hand, they exploit and sometimes maintain low costs and wages in those countries. And they often destroy or absorb smaller, weaker national competition. Most countries continue to welcome multinationals, but most now apply restrictions on how they operate.

Multinationals buy and sell in many different countries, so they are almost always very large. In certain commercial activities, for example, automobile manufacturing or pharmaceuticals, the cost of research and product development is enormous. There is probably no alternative to large multinational corporations in those areas. But the future does not have to be entirely multinational. Small- and medium-scale commercial activities can all be national or local. It mainly depends on the quality and efficiency of the national and local companies.

b Look at the company logos and answer the questions.

   1 What do you know about these companies?

   2 Which multinational corporations are in your country?

3 Listening

Look at the list of arrangements and
listen to the conversation. Write Kate
or Alex in the spaces.

1 Meet Dr. Chandry at airport: ....

2 Take him to hotel: ....

3 Have lunch with him: ....

4 Show him around Sydney: ....

4 Reading, writing and speaking

a Match the phrases in the box with the spaces in the e-mail.

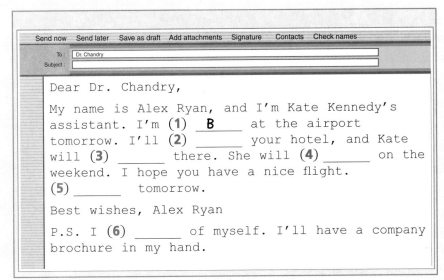

Send now   Send later   Save as draft   Add attachments   Signature   Contacts   Check names

To : Dr. Chandry
Subject :

Dear Dr. Chandry,

My name is Alex Ryan, and I'm Kate Kennedy's
assistant. I'm (**1**) __B__ at the airport
tomorrow. I'll (**2**) _____ your hotel, and Kate
will (**3**) _____ there. She will (**4**) _____ on the
weekend. I hope you have a nice flight.
(**5**) _____ tomorrow.

Best wishes, Alex Ryan

P.S. I (**6**) _____ of myself. I'll have a company
brochure in my hand.

A show you the sights
of Sydney

B ~~going to meet you~~

C See you

D have lunch with you

E attach a photo

F take you straight to

b Imagine that Dr. Chandry is going to visit your city.
Look at his details and use the information to plan
weekend activities for him. Write an e-mail to him
telling him about the plan.

c In pairs, exchange e-mails. Read your partner's e-mail.
Compare your plans for Dr. Chandry and decide on a final plan.

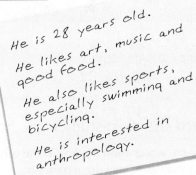

He is 28 years old.
He likes art, music and
good food.
He also likes sports,
especially swimming and
bicycling.
He is interested in
anthropology.

Unit 12 What's next?

1 Reviewing the situation

1 Reading, writing and speaking

a Read and complete this questionnaire with your personal information.

Topics	Questions		Answers
Study	1	Do you study now? If so, what?	
	2	Did you study 5 years ago? If so, what?	
Work	3	Do you work now? If so, what do you do?	
	4	Did you work 5 years ago? If so, what did you do?	
Home	5	Where do you live now?	
	6	Where did you live 5 years ago?	
Relationships	7	Are you dating / engaged / married now?	
	8	Were you dating / engaged / married 5 years ago?	
	9	Who are your best friends now?	
	10	Who were your best friends 5 years ago?	

b In groups, talk about the information in the questionnaire.

Things haven't changed much for me. I live in the same house. I have the same girlfriend. I ...

Things have changed a lot for me. I lived with my parents five years ago. Now I'm married, and I ...

2 Word builder: study, work, home, relationships

a Write the words from the box in the correct columns in the table. Check your answers with a partner.

Study	Work	Home	Relationships
class	employ	apartment	love

married   house   ~~employ~~   job
~~class~~   boss   ~~love~~   colleague
homework   kitchen   dictionary
engaged   housework   bedroom
course   school   wife   friend
boyfriend   ~~apartment~~   husband
office   salary   rent   lesson

b Complete the text with appropriate forms of the words from the box in exercise a.

Helen works in a large company. It (1).................... more than 1,500 people. She has an interesting (2)..................... with a good (3).................... . Peter is the sales manager in the same company. Helen and Peter are more than (4).................... at work. They are very much in (5).................... . They got (6).................... last year, and they are getting (7).................... next month. They have just rented an (8).................... in a nice neighborhood near the company. It has two (9).................... and a big living room. It's expensive, but they will have no problem paying the (10).................... with their combined income.

3 Speaking and listening

a Look at the photograph. In pairs, discuss the situation.

b Listen to the conversation. Then complete these sentences with Peter or Helen.

1 It's .... 's birthday.

2 .... is 28 years old.

3 .... is 27 at the moment.

4 It's .... 's photograph album.

5 .... has changed a lot since the age of 20.

6 .... hasn't changed much.

4 Pronunciation: sounds – /eɪ/

a Listen to these rhymes and repeat them.

1 Twenty-**eight** is not too **late**!   2 It's **great** to be twenty-**eight**!

b *Eight*, *late* and *great* contain the vowel sound /eɪ/, but are spelled in different ways. Underline more words in the box with the sound /eɪ/.

please	day	play	wait	came	way	height	neighbor	break
rain	fine	eat	clean	fly	right	mail	weight	either

c Listen to these words with different vowel sounds and spellings. Repeat them.

/eɪ/   neighbor, weight, late, came, great, break, day, wait

/i/   please, clean, eat, feet, green, complete

/aɪ/   height, right, light, fine, drive, fly, try

2 Immediate plans

1 Speaking and reading

a In groups, look at the photographs in the brochure. Which weekend break attracts you the most? Why?

b Read the brochure and the notes below. Choose the best weekend break for each person.

What are you doing next weekend? Nothing?
Well, choose one of our fantastic weekend breaks and get away!

Ⓐ White water rafting!

Two exciting days on one of the best rafting rivers in the country. Expert team leaders. Saturday night in a rustic chalet. You'll never forget the experience!

Ⓑ A romantic night!

A top class musical, plus dinner and Saturday night in a five star hotel – all for the price of the hotel room (double occupancy).

Ⓒ Chinese or English immersion programs!

Speak Chinese or English for three days (Friday – Sunday), in a beautiful country hotel! Learn while you relax in the country!

Emma:

Twenty-six years old, an engineer, single. Her company is sending her to their factory in Beijing for a year. She loves reading, hiking and swimming.

John:

Twenty-one years old, single, a computing student. He loves sports and physical activities. When he isn't in front of a computer screen, he's usually doing something outdoors.

David:

Twenty-four years old, an accountant, married. He works long hours. He and his wife, Barbara, a teacher, relax by listening to music. They both need a rest from their work.

c In groups, discuss the three weekend breaks, and agree on *one* for your whole group. Think about these questions and report your plan to the class.

1 What are you going to do?
2 Why are you going to do that, and not the other options?

2 Grammar builder: the future

a **Look at the sentences below and answer these questions.**

a) Which refers to a fixed arrangement, a plan / intention or a possibility?

b) Which verb structure is used for each?

1 She**'s going to** practice her Chinese on the weekend.

2 She already has her ticket. She**'s leaving** on the 7:15 plane on Saturday morning.

3 She **might stay** an extra night. It depends on her work schedule.

b **Complete these sentences with the verbs in parentheses. Check your answers with a partner.**

1 Claire and Barry .... (*get*) married next Sunday.

2 They .... (*have*) the reception in the garden. It depends on the weather.

3 They .... (*look for*) an apartment after the wedding.

4 Claire .... (*study*) French next year. It will be useful in her work.

5 Claire .... (*meet*) a French client this afternoon at 3:45.

6 The client .... (*speak*) English, but Claire isn't sure.

3 Listening and speaking

a **Listen to Sandra and Jake talking. What is their relationship?**

a) classmates   b) boyfriend and girlfriend   c) brother and sister

b **Look at the date books. Divide into two groups. Listen to the conversation again. Group A, complete Sandra's date book. Group B, complete Jake's date book.**

SANDRA'S DATE BOOK	JAKE'S DATE BOOK
Saturday a.m. **Tennis with Donna**	Saturday a.m. **Paint the front door**
Saturday p.m. _____	Saturday p.m. _____
Sunday a.m. _____	Sunday a.m. _____
Sunday p.m. _____	Sunday p.m. _____

c **In pairs (one person from group A and one from group B), check Sandra and Jake's plans.**

B: *What's Sandra going to do on Saturday morning?*

A: *She's playing tennis with Donna.*

d **In groups, discuss your arrangements, plans and possible activities for next week.**

3 Twenty-five years from now

1 Speaking and reading

a In pairs, match the words and phrases 1–8 with the phrases a–h.

1	expect	**a)**	be more than
2	exceed	**b)**	something you imagine, especially sleeping
3	literacy rates	**c)**	suddenly go up
4	slums	**d)**	be almost certain
5	jump	**e)**	video cassette recorders
6	take for granted	**f)**	the proportion of people able to read and write
7	VCRs	**g)**	very poor and dirty neighborhoods in cities
8	dream	**h)**	consider perfectly normal

b Read the article. In your opinion, does it correspond more to picture A, picture B or a combination of the two?

A look into the future

A person born in 1900 could expect to live about 36 years. Today, the global average is over 65, and by 2025 it is expected to exceed 72. The 20th century saw dramatic transformations in everything from medical care to literacy rates, and the changes will accelerate in the new millennium.

However, not all of them are good. The number of people living in slums, for instance, will jump from 810 million in 1995 to an estimated 2.1 billion in 2025. Many of the things we take for granted – e-mail, nuclear power, VCRs – weren't even a distant dream 100 years ago. The changes we saw in the last century will be insignificant in comparison to the ones we can expect to see in this one.

Here are some more facts about the past and estimates for the future:

	World population	People in cities	People in poverty	People per doctor
1995	5.8 billion	45%	2.4 billion	3,780
2025	8.5 billion	61%	3.3 billion	2,500

Adapted from: Newsweek, December 27, 1999–January 3, 2000

2 Speaking and listening

a In pairs, try to guess the answers for these predictions about 2025 in the U.S.

1 **a)** Twenty **b)** Thirty-five **c)** Fifty
   percent of the population will be Hispanic if immigration continues as at present.

2 **a)** Five **b)** Twenty-five **c)** Fifty
   percent of all adult Americans will be overweight.

3 **a)** Three **b)** Five **c)** Ten
   times more people will suffer from Alzheimer's if scientists don't discover a cure.

4 **a)** Medical research **b)** Computer technology
   c) Leisure and tourism will be the largest commercial activity.

5 Many more people will have
   a) cars **b)** pets **c)** houses.

b Listen to the radio program. Check your answers to exercise a.

3 Grammar builder: future with *will / won't*

a Look at these sentences. Do we use *will / won't* (*won't = will not*) for a) predictions or b) definite arrangements?

1 In twenty-five years, the number of people in slums will jump to over 2 billion.

2 Will there be many changes? Yes, there will.

3 Most people won't have a pet.

b Complete these sentences with *will* or *won't*, according to your opinions.

1 Children .... go to school.

2 People .... work in offices.

3 Computers .... be very different from computers now.

4 Most people .... be very fit.

5 Houses .... be bigger than they are now.

6 There .... be enough food for everyone in the world.

c In groups, compare your sentences.

4 Writing and speaking

a Write four or five predictions about your country in 2025. Use these phrases or your own ideas.

The capital city will ...
There won't be enough ...
Most children will ...
Most people our age will ...

b In groups, compare and discuss your predictions.

4 Lifeline to communications technology

1 Speaking and reading

a Look at the forms of international communication in the box. In groups, discuss the questions.

> Internet / e-mail   mail   telegraph / telegrams   telephone   radio

1 In 1900, what different ways existed for communication with people in other countries?

2 What different ways were there in 1980?

3 Do you ever communicate with people in other countries? If so, how?

b Read this extract and check your ideas about questions 1 and 2 in exercise a.

THE DEATH OF DISTANCE

Public mail service has existed for centuries, but telecommunications technology is also surprisingly old. By the 1870s, the world was linked by the electric telegraph. London was the center for most of the world's long-distance telegraphs, so English was the operating language. The invention of the telephone in 1876 made long-distance communication even more possible. However, cost was a major barrier to long-distance calls.

Since then the cost of communications has fallen dramatically. A three-minute telephone call between London and New York cost the equivalent of about $730 in 1928, and about 45¢ in 1998.

Prices have fallen mainly because of massive increases in demand and technological development. Today, undersea fiber-optic links can carry 600,000 simultaneous calls!

The Internet, established in 1991, uses the same infrastructure as the telephone. There is now probably more data traffic than voice traffic in the developed world. The vast majority of Internet communications are in English. The system has its origins in the scientific community, where English is the international lingua franca.

Adapted from: Graddol, D. 1997. *The Future of English?* The British Council

c In pairs, answer these questions.

1 Why was English the operating language of international telegraphy in the 19th century?

2 What was the great problem of international telephone calls in the first half of the 20th century?

3 Why are international telephone calls so cheap now compared with the past?

4 What communications technology does the Internet require?

5 Why is English the lingua franca of the Internet?

2 **Word builder:** connectors

a Look at these sentences. Which words indicate contrast? Which words indicate cause and result?

1 London was the relay center for telegraphs, **so** English was the operating language.

2 English was the operating language **because** London was the center for telegraphs.

3 The invention of the telephone made long-distance communication more possible. **However**, cost was a problem.

4 A lot of the traffic on the Internet is in English, **but** that will soon change.

b Write these sentences in a different way but don't change the meaning. Use *because*, *but*, *however* or *so*. Check your answers with a partner.

1 The mail has existed for centuries, but telecommunications technology is also old.

2 Prices have fallen because communications technology has developed enormously.

3 A call between London and New York was very expensive in 1928. However, today the cost is almost zero.

4 The Internet has its origins in the scientific community, so English is the main language.

> **Language assistant**
> *However* and *but* are equivalent, but *however* is more formal.

3 **Speaking**

Look at the pictures. In groups, discuss these questions.

1 Which technologies already exist?

2 Which technologies are probable soon?

3 Which device would you most like to have?

A *Computer translation*

B *Cellular vision-phone*

C *Automatic interpreter*

D *Voice-controlled computer*

Checkpoint 6

1 Check your progress

a Complete the e-mail with the correct forms of the verbs in parentheses. You may need to add other words.

Send now   Send later   Save as draft   Add attachments   Signature   Contacts   Check names

To : Karen

Subject :

Hi Karen,

Thanks for your mail. How are you? Well I **(1)**_____ (finish) college in June and I **(2)**_____ (work) in a restaurant for a month to make some money. When I finish I **(3)**_____ (take) a vacation. I haven't finalized my plans, but I **(4)** _____ (go) to California. A friend of mine **(5)**_____ (get married) on August 17 and he invited me to the wedding. I haven't been to California but at the moment I **(6)**_____ (learn) how to surf to impress my friends!

It's not definite but I **(7)**_____ (come) to Seattle. Are you **(8)**_____ (be) there? Let me know and maybe we can meet.

All the best, Eric

b Read the interview from a company magazine and fill in the spaces with a suitable word.

Daybreak Information Systems, Fresno, California.

Employee of the month – Sara Garcia

Interviewer: (9) _____ long have you (10) _____ for the company?

Sara: (11) _____ 1996. I started work in the sales area and now I'm Marketing Manager.

Interviewer: Have you always (12) _____ in the U.S.?

Sara: No. I was (13) _____ in Colombia, but my parents (14) _____ to Miami, Florida when I (15) _____ three years old. My parents still (16) _____ in Miami.

Interviewer: And what (17) _____ you study in college?

Sara: My major was business administration.

Interviewer: And (18) _____ did you come to California?

Sara: After college for my first job. I've been here (19) _____ six years and I love it.

Interviewer: What about your interests and hobbies?

Sara: Well, I love going to see movies and playing the piano. I've (20) _____ the piano since I was a kid.

Score out of 20

○ 18–20 Excellent!   ○ 15–17 Very good!   ○ 12–14 OK, but review.   ○ 9–11 You have some problems. Review units 11 and 12.   ○ 0–8 Talk to your teacher.

2 Games to play

a In groups, play the "But, so game." One person invents the first line of a story. The line finishes with the word "but." The second person continues the story and finishes with the word "so." Continue the story in your group.

A: I bought an elephant, but ...
B: I bought an elephant, but it was too big to take on the bus so ...
C: I bought an elephant, but it was too big to take on the bus so I took a taxi, but ...

b In two teams, take turns choosing a word or expression from the box. The other team makes a sentence using *do* or *make*. Give two points for a correct sentence.

Team A: An excuse.
Team B: He made an excuse.
Team A: Correct! Two points.

homework	a mistake	breakfast
your best	a good job	cookies
~~excuse~~	a favor	some coffee
exercise	a mess	a lot of money

3 Your world

Complete the table with information about you. Then interview a partner using *How long ...?* or *When ...?* and complete the "Your partner" column.

When were you born? How long have you lived in your house?

Topic	You	Your partner
born		
live in your present house / apartment		
meet your best friend		
have your job / be in college		
get your first job		
study English		

4 Personal word bank

Add more words that are important to you. Compare your lists with a partner.

Home	Work	Relationships	Phrases
bedroom	office	colleague	How long have you lived here?

Songsheet 1
I say a little prayer

1 Speaking

a Match the things in the picture with the words in the box.

> pajamas   a comb   make up
> a razor   a shower   a brush
> an alarm clock   a toothbrush

b Talk about the picture. What else can you see?

2 Vocabulary: collocation

a Match the verbs to the correct nouns. There are two nouns for each verb.

b Can you add any other nouns used with these verbs?

3 Speaking

a **What do you do in the morning? Choose from this list.**

1 wake up
2 get up
3 put on make up
4 shave
5 comb / brush your hair

6 run for the bus / train
7 take a shower / bath
8 say a prayer
9 have breakfast
10 get dressed

b **What else do you do? Add two more things to the list.**

c **Compare your answers with a partner.**

I never / sometimes / always / usually ...

4 Listening

a **Listen to the song and check (✓) what the person does in the morning from the list in exercise 3a.**

b **Listen again and read the song lyrics. Check your answers.**

I say a little prayer

The moment I wake up
Before I put on my make up
I say a little prayer for you.
While combing my hair now,
And wondering what dress to wear now
I say a little prayer for you.

Forever, forever, you'll stay in my heart
And I will love you
Forever, forever, we never will part
Oh, how I'll love you
Together, together, that's how it must be
To live without you
Would only be heartbreak for me.

I run for the bus, dear,
While riding I think of us, dear,

I say a little prayer for you.
At work I just take time
And all through my coffee break-time
I say a little prayer for you.

Forever, forever, you'll stay in my heart
And I will love you
Forever, forever, we never will part
Oh, how I'll love you
Together, together, that's how it must be
To live without you
Would only be heartbreak for me.

My darling, believe me
For there is no-one
But you.
Please love me true, coz I'm in love with you.
Answer my prayer, say you'll love me true.

5 Vocabulary and speaking

a **Work in groups. Say what you do in the evening. Make a list.**

b **Show your list to another group. Compare your answers.**

have dinner,
have a bath,

Songsheet 2
The girl from Ipanema

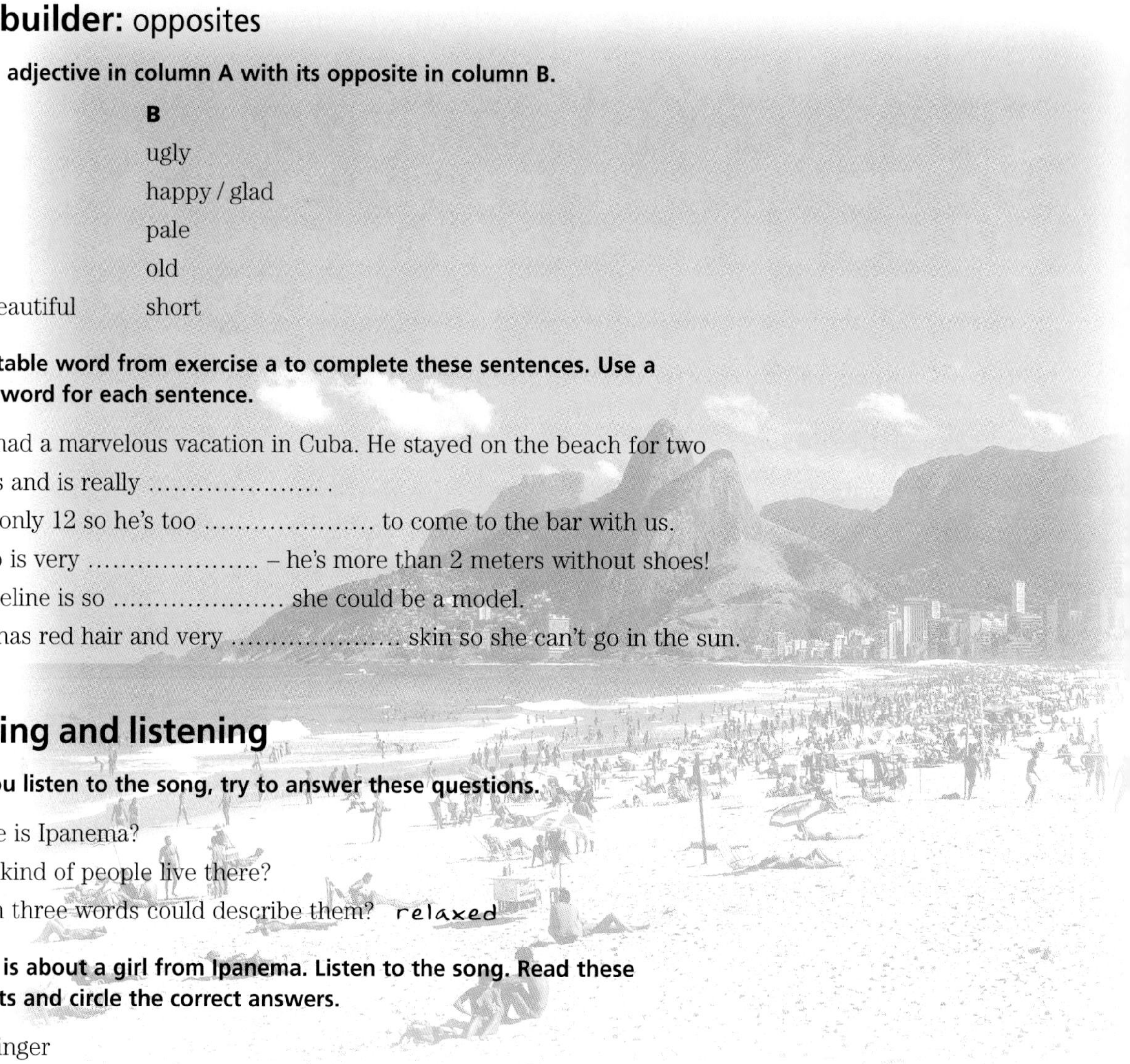

1 Word builder: opposites

a Match an adjective in column A with its opposite in column B.

A	B
tall	ugly
tan	happy / glad
young	pale
sad	old
lovely / beautiful	short

b Use a suitable word from exercise a to complete these sentences. Use a different word for each sentence.

1 Joao had a marvelous vacation in Cuba. He stayed on the beach for two weeks and is really ....

2 Gil is only 12 so he's too .... to come to the bar with us.

3 Pietro is very .... – he's more than 2 meters without shoes!

4 Jacqueline is so .... she could be a model.

5 Sally has red hair and very .... skin so she can't go in the sun.

2 Speaking and listening

a Before you listen to the song, try to answer these questions.

1 Where is Ipanema?

2 What kind of people live there?

3 Which three words could describe them? *relaxed*

b The song is about a girl from Ipanema. Listen to the song. Read these statements and circle the correct answers.

1 The singer

a) knows the girl from Ipanema **b)** doesn't know her

2 The singer is feeling

a) happy **b)** sad

3 The girl in the song

a) is exceptionally beautiful **b)** is normal looking

The girl from Ipanema

Tall and tan and young and lovely
The girl from Ipanema goes walking
And when she passes each one she passes goes – ah.

When she walks she's like a samba
That swings so cool and sways so gently
That when she passes each one she passes goes – ooh.

Ooh but he watches so sadly
How can he tell her he loves her
Yes he would give his heart gladly but each day when she walks to the sea
She looks straight ahead, not at he.

Tall and tan and young and lovely
The girl from Ipanema goes walking
And when she passes, he smiles – but she doesn't see.
She just doesn't see.

c   Listen again and read the lyrics. Check your answers to exercise b.

3 Writing and reading

a   Below is a personal advertisement that a man wrote. Is this man a good date for the girl from Ipanema?

PHYSICAL DESCRIPTION
Favorite color and personality: I'm single and 85 years old. I am bald and have blue eyes. I'm not very sociable, but I am very energetic. Red's my favorite color!

LIKES AND DISLIKES
Leisure activities: I don't like modern music, but I love classical music and doing housework! I like riding my old Harley Davidson motorcycle and

swimming – I always swim 15 kilometers a day.

PLANS
I'm flying to India next month. Want to come?

b   Now imagine that you are a girl or boy from Ipanema. Write a personal advertisement about yourself. Look at exercise a to help you.

c   Put your advertisement on the wall. Read the other advertisements and find a partner.

4 Speaking

a   In pairs, imagine you are going to meet the girl or boy from Ipanema. It's your first date. Plan the conversation.

b   Change pairs and have the conversation.

   Hello, I'm …

Songsheet 3
Daniel

1 Speaking

a Look at these phrases. Put them in the order they usually happen.

- ◯ The plane takes off.
- ◯ Get on the plane.
- ◯ Check in at the airport.
- ◯ Go to the airport.
- ◯ The plane lands.

Quick, follow that plane!

b Put these pictures in the correct order and use the phrases from exercise 1a to talk about what is happening.

2 Speaking and listening

a In pairs, look at these sentences and listen to the song. As you listen, circle which words are true from the song.

1 Daniel is travelling by *plane / boat / train*.
2 Daniel is going to *Spain / England / Mexico*.
3 *He has been there before / This is his first visit.*
4 Daniel is *older / younger* than the singer.
5 They are *brothers / friends / father and son*.

b Now listen to the song again and check your answers.

Daniel

Daniel is traveling tonight on a plane
I can see the red tail lights heading for Spain
Oh, and I can see Daniel waving goodbye
God, it looks like Daniel, must be the clouds in my eyes.

They say Spain is pretty though I've never been
Daniel says it's the best place he's ever seen
Oh, and he should know, he's been there enough
Lord, I miss Daniel, oh I miss him so much.

Daniel, my brother, you are older than me
Do you still feel the pain of the scars that won't heal
Your eyes have died but you see more than I
Daniel, you're a star in the face of the sky.

Daniel is traveling tonight on a plane
I can see the red tail lights heading for Spain
Oh, and I can see Daniel waving goodbye
God, it looks like Daniel, must be the clouds in my eyes
God, it looks like Daniel, must be the clouds in my eyes.

c In groups, discuss these questions with reference to the song.

1 How does the singer feel about his brother?
2 How does the singer feel about his brother leaving?
3 What are the clouds in the singer's eyes?

3 Pronunciation: rhyme

Close your books and listen to the song again. Write down the words
that rhyme.

4 Writing and speaking

Complete these sentences about yourself. Then tell a partner.

1 I like travelling by ....
2 I'd like to go to ....
3 I've (never) been to ....
4 My best vacation was ....
5 I remember saying goodbye to my ....
   at the .... It was ....

Songsheet 4
Till there was you

1 Vocabulary

a Work with a partner and find these things in the pictures.

1 a bell   5 a meadow
2 a hill   6 people singing
3 a bird   7 dawn
4 a rose

b What other things can you see in the pictures?

c Now match the words in the columns.

bell	smell
bird	ring
music	play
flowers	sing

2 Speaking and listening

a The words and pictures from exercises 1a and c are from a song. What is it about?

b Listen to the song and match each of the four verses with one of the things in the pictures.

Till there was you

There were bells on a hill
But I never heard them ringing
No, I never heard them at all
Till there was you.

There were birds in the sky
But I never saw them winging
No, I never saw them at all
Till there was you.

Then there was music and wonderful roses
They tell me – in sweet fragrant meadows
Of dawn and dew.

There was love all around
But I never heard it singing
No, I never heard it at all
Till there was you.

Then there was music and wonderful roses
They tell me – in sweet fragrant meadows
Of dawn and dew.

There was love all around
But I never heard it singing
No, I never heard it at all
Till there was you.

3 Speaking

Discuss these questions about the lyrics of the song.

1 What was life like before the singer fell in love?
2 What was life like after the singer fell in love?
3 How do people change when they fall in love?

4 Writing and reading

a Write your own verse by completing the spaces with your ideas.

There was / were .... ,
But I never .... ,
No, I never .... it / them at all
Till ....

There was a hole in the street,
But I never saw it coming,
No, I never saw it at all
Till I fell in.

b Put your verses up on the wall. Read them and then discuss these questions.

1 Which is the funniest?
2 Which is the most romantic?
3 Which is the craziest?
4 Which is the best?

Songsheet 5
The sweetest feeling

1 Vocabulary: opposites

a Match the opposites in the box with the pictures.

far	sweet
deep	close
~~shallow~~	sour

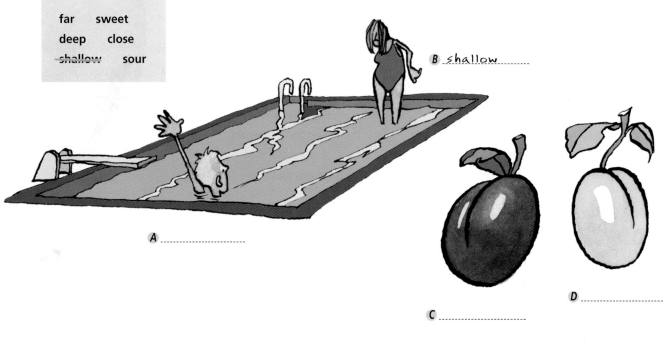

B shallow

A ....

D ....

C ....

E ....   *F* ....

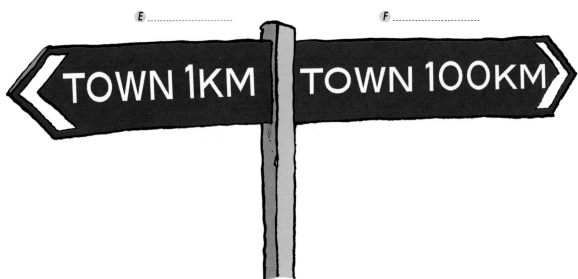

b Form the comparatives of the words from exercise a.

far – farther than

2 Listening

a Listen to the song. How does the singer feel?

b Listen again and put the words and pictures in the order that they are in the song.

1–D

The sweetest feeling

The closer you get, the better you look, baby
The better you look, the more I want you
When you turn on your smile
You make my heart go wild
I'm like a child with a brand new toy
And I get the sweetest feeling, loving you.

The warmer your kiss
The deeper you touch me, baby
The deeper you touch, the more you thrill me
It's more than I can stand
Girl, when you hold my hand
I feel so grand that I could cry
And I get the sweetest feeling, loving you.

The greater your love, the closer you hold me
The closer you hold, the more I need you
With every passing day
I love you more in every way
I'm in love to stay and I wanna say …
And I get the sweetest feeling, loving you.

3 Writing and reading

a In this song, the man is in love. Imagine that after some time, he doesn't feel in love any more! In pairs, rewrite part of the song to show his new feelings.

The closer you get the worse you look, baby
The worse you look, the more I hate you!!

b Read other classmates' versions. Choose the best one. If you want to, you can sing it!

Songsheet 6
Holiday

1 Vocabulary: words with similar meanings

a Match words with similar meanings together.

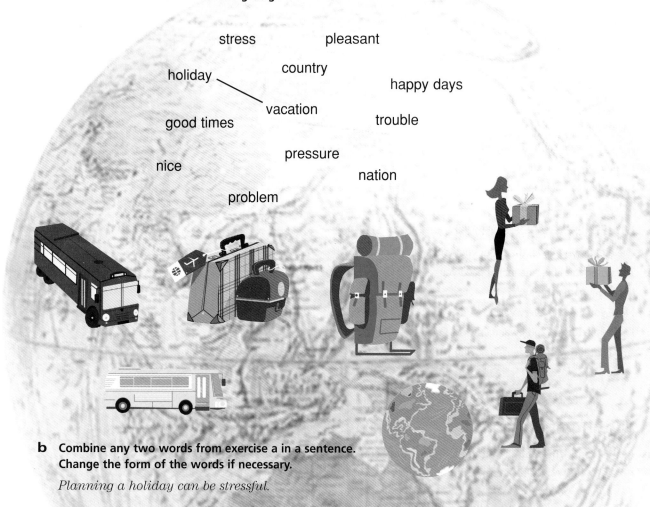

stress   pleasant

holiday   country

happy days

vacation

trouble

good times

nice   pressure

nation

problem

b Combine any two words from exercise a in a sentence.
Change the form of the words if necessary.

Planning a holiday can be stressful.

2 Pronunciation and word building

a Notice the spelling and stress pattern of these words.

educate	edu**ca**tion	**de**monstrate	demon**stra**tion
celebrate	cele**bra**tion	**con**centrate	concen**tra**tion
indicate	indi**ca**tion	**to**lerate	toler**a**tion

b Can you think of more examples of this pattern? Check
with a partner or your dictionary.

3 Listening and reading

a Listen to the song and check (✓) the words that you hear.

- ◯ holiday
- ◯ celebrate
- ◯ demonstrate
- ◯ good times
- ◯ sad days
- ◯ revolution
- ◯ nation
- ◯ bad times

b Now read the lyrics as you listen to the song again. Check your answers.

Holiday

Holiday, celebrate
Holiday, celebrate
If we took a holiday
Took some time to celebrate
Just one day out of life
It would be, it would be so nice.

Everybody spread the word
We're gonna have a celebration.
All across the world
In every nation
It's time for the good times
Forget about the bad times, oh yeah.
One day to come together
To release the pressure
We need a holiday.

You can turn this world around
And bring back all of those happy days.
Put your troubles down
It's time to celebrate.
Let love shine
And we will find
A way to come together
And make things better
We need a holiday.

Holiday, celebrate
Holiday, celebrate

Holiday, celebrate
Holiday, celebrate

Holiday, celebration
Come together in every nation.

4 Writing and speaking

a In groups, discuss these statements and then complete them with the group's ideas. Compare your answers with another group.

1 Family vacations are important because …
2 Vacations with friends are important because …
3 National festivals are important because …

b In groups, invent a festival for the world. It should be truly universal. Make notes on the following ideas.

1 reason for the festival
2 type of dress for the festival
3 type of music and food for the festival
4 location for the first year of the festival and why
5 date and name for the festival

c Present your world festival to the class. Which group has the best idea?

Irregular verbs

Infinitive	Past	Past participle	Unit and lesson
be	was / were	been	U1, L1
become	became	become	U6, L1
begin	began	begun	U2, L1
blow	blew	blown	U6, L3
break	broke	broken	U10, L3
bring	brought	brought	U8, L1
build	built	built	U8, L1
buy	bought	bought	U2, L2
can	could	could	U2, L3
choose	chose	chosen	U1, L2
come	came	come	U6, L4
do	did	done	U1, L1
drink	drank	drunk	U11, L1
drive	drove	driven	U6, L2
eat	ate	eaten	U2, L2
fall	fell	fallen	U6, L1
feel	felt	felt	U4, L4
find	found	found	U4, L4
fly	flew	flown	U4, L3
forget	forgot	forgotten	U8, L3
freeze	froze	frozen	U11, L1
get	got	gotten	U1, L3
give	gave	given	U3, L3
go	went	gone	U1, L4
grow	grew	grown	U6, L1
have	had	had	U1, L2
hear	heard	heard	U6, L2
hit	hit	hit	U6, L1
keep	kept	kept	U9, L1

Infinitive	Past	Past participle	Unit and lesson
know	knew	known	U1, L2
leave	left	left	U2, L1
lend	lent	lent	Checkpoint 4
let	let	let	U4, L4
lose	lost	lost	U4, L4
make	made	made	U2, L1
mean	meant	meant	U4, L1
meet	met	met	U2, L4
put	put	put	U6, L1
read	read	read	U1, L2
run	ran	run	U1, L3
say	said	said	U1, L3
see	saw	seen	U6, L3
send	sent	sent	U2, L1
sit	sat	sat	Checkpoint 2
sleep	slept	slept	U6, L3
speak	spoke	spoken	U1, L2
spend	spent	spent	U4, L4
steal	stole	stolen	U6, L3
swim	swam	swum	Checkpoint 3
take	took	taken	U2, L1
teach	taught	taught	U7, L4
tell	told	told	U2, L4
think	thought	thought	U3, L4
wear	wore	worn	Checkpoint 2
win	won	won	U2, L2
write	wrote	written	U1, L1
understand	understood	understood	U8, L3

Pronunciation chart

Vowels

[i]	eat
[ɪ]	sit
[eɪ]	wait
[e]	get
[æ]	hat
[aɪ]	write
[ʌ]	but
[u:]	food
[ʊ]	good
[oʊ]	go
[ɔ:]	saw
[a]	hot
[aʊ]	cow
[ɔɪ]	boy
[iər]	here
[ər]	her
[eər]	hair
[or]	or
[ar]	far

Consonants
(shown as initial sounds)

[b]	bat
[k]	cat
[tʃ]	chair
[d]	dog
[f]	fat
[g]	girl
[h]	hat
[dʒ]	July
[k]	coat
[l]	like
[m]	man
[n]	new
[p]	pet
[kw]	queen
[r]	run
[s]	see
[ʃ]	shirt
[t]	talk
[ð]	the
[θ]	thin
[v]	voice
[w]	where
[j]	you
[ŋ]	sing (as final sound)
[z]	zoo

The alphabet

/eɪ/	/i/	/e/	/aɪ/	/oʊ/	/u:/	/ar/
Aa	Bb	Ff	Ii	Oo	Qq	Rr
Hh	Cc	Ll	Yy		Uu	
Jj	Dd	Mm			Ww	
Kk	Ee	Nn				
	Gg	Ss				
	Pp	Xx				
	Tt					
	Vv					
	Zz					

Macmillan Education
Between Towns Road, Oxford, OX4 3PP
A division of Macmillan Publishers Limited
Companies and representatives throughout the world

ISBN 978 0 333 92674 1

Text © Simon Brewster, Paul Davies, Mickey Rogers 2001
Songsheets written by Kate Fuscoe

Design and illustration © Macmillan Publishers Limited 2001

First published 2001

Designed by Anne Sherlock, based on original design by Kevin Mcgeoghegan

Illustrated by Martin Ashton, Red Giraffe, Rob Loxton, Sue Potter,
Gavin Reece, Paul Scholfield, Andy Warrington, Geoff Waterhouse

Cover photograph by Stone

The publishers would like to thank the following for reading the
material and making comments: María Inês Albernaz, English Teacher,
Centro Federal de Educação Tecnológica, CEFET-Campos, Brazil and
English Teacher, Instituto Brasil, Estados Unidos de Campos, Brazil;
Florinda Scremin Marquez, ELT/ESP Professor and Coordinator, FESP,
Curitiba, Brazil; Vládia María Cabral Borges, Professor of English
Linguistics and Applied Linguistics, Head of Department of Foreign
Languages, University of Ceará, Forteleza, Brazil; Monica Myers, English
in Action, São Paulo, Brazil; Luís Manuel Malta de Alves Louceiro,
Coordinator, ESL Institute, English at Sabin, São Paulo, Brazil; Ricardo
Romero-Medina, Associate Professor, Foreign Languages Department,
Universidad Nacional de Colombia, Bogotá, Colombia; Clara Inês García,
Head of Language Center, Universidad Militar Nueva Granada, Bogotá;
María Teresa Barrera Castillo, Department of Languages, Universidad
Veracruzana, Mexico; Alina Blanco, UPEAP University, Puebla, Mexico;
Jean-Pierre Brossard, Academic Director, Proulex, Guadalajara, Mexico;
Teresa Castineira, English Teacher, Benemérita Universidad Autónoma de
Puebla, Mexico; Adriana Lucía Patricia Dorantes González, Head of
Languages Department, Universidad Autónoma Agraria, Saltillo, Mexico;
Albina Escobar, Freelance Teacher Trainer and Consultant, Brazil;
Norma Duarte Martinez, English Coordinator, Veterinary Medicine and
Husbandry College, Universidad Nacional Autónoma de México,
Coyoacan, Mexico; Carol Lethaby, ELT Teacher Trainer/Consultant,
Department of Modern Languages, Universidad de Guadalajara/The
British Council, Mexico; Connie Rae Johnson, Professor and Teacher,
Universidad de las Américas, Puebla, Mexico; Vera Lucía Lovato Bruno,
Director and Teacher, Vertex Express English Course, Brazil.

Picture research by Penni Bickle

Commissioned photographs by Yiorgos Nikiteas pp 6,8(t),10,11,22,25,29
(abc&f),31,34(m),53(b),61,69,76(t),88,98,99,105. Haddon Davis p14.

The authors and publishers would like to thank the following for permission
to reproduce their photographs:
Allsport pp81,86, Mason 90; Mason 90;Bayer pp102; Corbis pp24(b),
Jordice 115; David Simson pp48, 52(m), 85, 96(br), 121; Eye
Ubiquitous George pp16, Forman 71(l), Nasa74(b), J Burke 85(tl & c),
Seheult 96(l); Hulton Getty pp35, 68 (1) (3) (4) (a) (c) (d), 92(tl),
92(m); Ian Howell pp92(tr); James Davis Travel Photography pp8(m),
17, 20(2), 20(3),32(t),85(tr),106(l),116; Kobal pp50(l), 54, 87, 94;
Library of Congress/Bridgeman Art Library pp75(b); Mary Evans
pp68(b); Massachusetts Institute of Technology pp62; Magnum/ Nicols
pp 42, S Perkins 92(l); Penni Bickle pp85(r), 97; Pictor pp 26(l),30, 85,
106(m), 125; Picture Bank pp79; Powerstock pp74(t), 78,119; Retna
pp50(r); Rex Features pp50(b); Ronald Grant pp84(poster); Science
Picture Library/ Eye of Science pp84(t); Shell pp102; South American
Pictures pp71(m & r); Spectrum pp18, M Putland 63(bl), G Peress
63(br); Telegraph Colour Library / Rawlings/pp 8(Golden Gate), 20 (l),
Goldman 24(t), Bildagentur 26(r), 75 (t),V C L 27(l), 29 (t), 84 (l),
100(l), Chappel 27(m), Chernus 27(r), Cuthbert G Buss 32(m),
Brimson 53, Benelux 67 (tl), Sherman 67 (bl), E Taylor 67 (br), M
Malyszko100(r), Capucine117; Tony Stone pp85, Kingsworth 15, Cohen
21, Craus 36, Sherman 36, Dolding 37, Day 79(t) Thompson&Thompson
32(b); Winston Fraser pp63(tr),97(t); ZEFA pp34 (l & r); Zul pp 8 (b),
67(tl), 85(tr), 106(r),Knights 29(d),52(l).

The publishers would like to thank EF International School of English,
Brighton; the Beach Hotel, Brighton; Direct Residential Lettings Ltd,
Hove; and Madison Travel, Hove.

Among all the people who contributed to the Skyline project, the authors
give special thanks to John Waterman and Manuela Lima, who did much
more than their duty as editors. Thank you, John and Manuela! The
authors would also like to thank Katie Austin for the cover designs.

Printed in Thailand.

2012 2011 2010 2009 2008
15   14   13   12   11